You Can Pass
Any Bar Exam

You Can Pass Any Bar Exam

Edna Wells Handy

Law Professor
Former Federal District Court Law Clerk
Former Assistant United States Attorney
Former Assistant District Attorney

Admitted: New York, 9th Cir.,
U.S. Sup. Ct., SDNY

Practising Law Insitute
New York City
K1-1600

ISBN: 0-87224-105-X

TABLE OF CONTENTS

Preface

TO MICHAEL
KENYA, JANNAH AND JACQUELINE

PREFACE

"Pumpernickel bagel with cream cheese;
extra light coffee, two sugars, please."

This was my Monday to Friday supper for the weeks I attended bar review. I ordered this meal around the same time each day. At the bar review lecture hall, I ate this same meal at the same seat, next to the same friend. I took notes in the same notebook, using the same format. I caught the train and bus at the same time and at the same locations. I went to sleep at night and got up each morning at the same time and in the same place.

You would think that all this *sameness* would have made those weeks pretty dreadful. They weren't. While I would not go so far as to say it was an exciting period of my life, I will say that the sameness created a level of comfort, predictability and, more surprisingly, control during an otherwise intimidating time. Although I came to the bar exam not really knowing what to expect (much like first year), the fact that I had ordered my life down to the detail of what my nightly meal would be, gave me the confidence of knowing that I could handle whatever *they* threw at me.

I have been teaching people how to pass the bar exam for almost 16 years. I did not know it then, but the approach which I encourage students to adopt is a tested and refined version of what I developed for my own bar exam. I call it *The Program*. Simply put, *The Program* is the means by which students can best learn all of the required subjects for the bar while keeping their personal and professional lives intact and maintaining their sanity during the weeks of preparation.

I have found over time that *The Program* not only works for the bar exam, it can work to meet many of life's challenges. It was the means and method by which I passed the bar, litigated complex criminal cases, directed the research, writing and publication of a 2,000-page commission report, and, finally, wrote and published this book. Even with *The Program*, however, none of this would have been possible without the love, support and guidance which I received from my family (especially my mother), mentors and friends.

I know that *The Program* can work for you. If you adopt its dual approach, success will be yours. Throughout this manual I present that approach.

It is discussed in detail in the first chapter, in a step-by-step presentation of what you need to do to prepare for the mental challenge of the exam. Your mental attitude plays as much a part in passing as does your learning the law. As part of this mental preparation, I discuss the importance of demystifying the exam itself in Chapter Two.

Subsequent chapters present my thesis that a well-ordered life and study regimen will lead to a well-written bar exam essay answer. Chapter Six, perhaps the one you will seek out, discusses the mechanics of writing that well-written essay answer, along with choosing that *best* Multistate Bar Examination answer and *correct* multiple choice answer.

Whether you elect to take a review course or not, the next chapter lays out options and strategies for going it alone or choosing the best course for you. Chapter Eight, entitled *Not For the Minority Student Only*, goes beyond the statistics on minority performance on the exam to get to root causes for any variances between groups. In so doing, I present strategies for success which all students who have real or perceived *special* needs can adopt to meet those challenges. Chapters Nine and Ten address particular concerns, like whether you should take two exams or how to avoid the scheduling crunch students often face a month into the study period. I give my *two cents* on taking two exams and suggest techniques for avoiding the crunch.

Failing the exam can be a most devastating event. Repeated failures can zap energy, confidence, and finances. There are reasons why people fail and ways to stop the cycle of failure or prevent one from starting. Chapter Eleven details those reasons and those strategies.

No matter which bar exam you take, this manual can be of significant assistance. While I sometimes use the law or sample bar exam questions from specific jurisdictions to illustrate a point, you can use the information given here whether you sit for the New York, Virgin Islands, Indiana or California bar exam. It matters not whether you are a first-time taker, a repeater or someone already in practice but in need of admission to a different state. ***If you adopt The Program, you can pass any bar exam.***

Edna Wells Handy
Brooklyn, 1995

CHAPTER ONE

THE PROGRAM

When we sit alone to study for the bar exam, many of us hear negative voices: "No, you can't." "It's impossible." "It can't be done." To avoid these thoughts, we avoid the situation, in this case, the studying, and we thereby lessen our chances of passing. I say, "Do not avoid the thoughts. Control and conquer them." By adopting *The Program*, you can.

The Program concentrates on two aspects of your life, your attitude and discipline. It teaches you how to develop a positive attitude and how to manage your life effectively to reach your intended goal of passing the bar exam.

The "Yes I Can" Attitude

You've heard it said in so many ways: "The power of positive thinking"; "possibility thinking"; "creative imagining." It is more than simply an idea. Put into action, it could be just the approach you need to remove self-inhibiting notions that you *can't* pass this exam. The *Yes I Can* way of thinking will do this. For every disaffirming thought, there is a self-affirming notion. To meet destructive action, enlist constructive energy. To neutralize thoughts of failing, visualize scenes of passing. Here are the steps.

Step One: You must engage in creative imagining by visualizing the goal of the bar exam process, *passing.* Before you begin studying, close your eyes and visualize the front page of the newspaper announcing the pass rates for the exam you are about to take. Go to the page of the article where you would expect to find your name, e.g., New York lists names of successful candidates in alphabetical order under the department to which they seek admission. See your name in print. It will be your last name followed by your first name and middle initial.

Now, begin to plan your celebration to start the minute the exam is over. Plan your evening out after the last day of the exam. Go to a party, dinner, a movie, an amusement park. Next, plan a trip. It matters not where you go, just as long as you get away for awhile. Get brochures, pamphlets, a list of places you want to visit, and visualize yourself there, "foot loose and fancy free." You will have earned it.

Step Two: Go back to the beginning of this mental process and let yourself think about failing. However, you are allowed to think about it only once! Then, as they say, "Perish the thought." Each time the thought seeks resurrection, meet it head-on with the image of your name in the paper, your party and your trip. Try a device some athletes use. Write *Yes I can* notes to yourself and conspicuously place them in your home or office.

Step Three: Keep away from negative thinking and speaking people, especially those in your family. First, tell them that you are going to pass; that you would appreciate their support; but if not, you would appreciate their silence on the matter. If you must live in a non-affirming environment during this period, stay out of it for as long as you can. Be there only when those creating that atmosphere are not.

Step Four: Surround yourself with positive thinking and speaking people, not flatterers, just people who find it easier to praise than to condemn, who elevate rather than deflate and who encourage as opposed to discourage. All you need is one or two such people. Keep a motivational tape or book handy to help you to maintain a positive outlook. See *Appendix A* for a listing. Contact The Legal Skills Center at (212) 332-0832 for the telephone number of a motivational "hot-line." The positive support and encouragement you need is there, it is in you and around you. Sometimes it is just a matter of being open to the possibilities. Sometimes it is just a matter of how you choose to look at things.

Is the exam a torturous ordeal
or a time of professional growth?

The bar exam and its preparation time test a person's mettle and give insight into an individual's personality, life and very being. Most often, we hear of the exam and the preparation for it as being necessary evils: the pits, torture. I urge you, however, to view the exam and the study process leading up to it as a huge step forward in your growth as a lawyer. The practice of law is ruled by the very same details, minutia and deadlines you must learn for the bar exam. Law practice is also marked by the same peaks and valleys in preparation and presentation as you will find in studying for the bar exam, and often requires the same quick analysis of issues to determine legal implications. Preparation for the bar exam and the exam itself, in their own way, can help you to become a better lawyer.

Step Five: Many students think that there is a bar review course, school or study technique *out there* that will enable them to pass the bar exam. These things help but most of what you need is already *inside of you*!

Jerome B.

Jerry had heard one of my lectures and requested private tutoring. He was a first-time taker and was beginning to obsess over whether he would pass. He really did not know why he was so unnerved. After all, he had gone to an Ivy League law school and college and he had always done well.

After we talked a bit, Jerry mentioned that he had once been overweight by 50 lbs. He told me that he had religiously followed a weight reduction program for almost a year to lose the initial pounds and now was pretty conscientious about watching his weight to stay trim.[1]

I seized upon this information to allay Jerry's fear, explaining to

---

[1]All case studies represent a composite of the challenges candidates face. Any similarity to persons alive or deceased is purely coincidental.

him that he already knew what he needed to pass. By choosing the goal of losing weight, meticulously watching his diet, unfailingly participating in a support group, and inhibiting his thoughts and cravings, he had developed the type of self-discipline needed to pass the bar exam.

*   *   *

We all have a success story.   Your success may have come about through a step-by-step program as presented here or through your own process and creativity. A large part of what I do in my own bar review tutoring is to identify for my students their own personal experiences to show them that they already possess the intellectual, physical and spiritual resources needed to turn any major project like the bar exam into a vehicle for personal growth and success. These successes show that we already have a blueprint for passing the bar. All we need do is to recognize it and build upon it.

Whatever the approach, a similar theme will run through the successful ones. **Discipline**: the discipline which allows you to concentrate and to pay attention to the *detail*; be it the *detail* in measuring your food in a weight-watching program or the *detail* in determining whether you count holidays when calculating the number of days in which to answer a summons and complaint. Our program calls upon that discipline. It develops and strenghtens it by directing all of our energies into a single focus, passing the bar.

In the face of thoughts of failing the bar exam, the *Yes I Can* attitude and discipline encouraged by **the Program** show you how to ward off such thoughts by focusing on past successes and reminding yourself of times when you said, **"Yes I can" . . . and did!**

CHAPTER TWO

DEMYSTIFYING THE BAR EXAM

Imagine yourself the day before the bar exam. You are too excited to sleep, but you make yourself do so anyway. You have chosen your clothes for the next day. You know your travel route and an alternative in case of emergencies. You feel good. You feel ready. You feel confident. And yes, you are a little anxious. But you have stayed on your schedule. Your body is in relatively good working order. You have absorbed so much information that you can actually visualize pages of text from your study outline. Are you having trouble imaging this?

I tell students all the time that the bar exam will be one of the easier exams they will ever take because of the simple fact that there are *correct* or *best* answers, based upon objective, verifiable law. Yet, few of them believe me. When given the choice, too many bar candidates would rather think about the exam in skeptical, even fatalistic terms. They choose to do so because of the tendency to view the bar exam in insolation; as if it were separate from the process which the candidate had begun in the first year of law school. The process of becoming an attorney.

If you can think of the exam as a part of that process, one which will bring you closer to your goal of becoming an attorney, one that will leave you with skills and knowledge you will find useful for the practice of law, then the bar exam will not loom as some large, insurmountable obstacle. It will merely be the next logical step in your development.

By adopting *the Program*, you can turn your thinking around. *The Program* will require that you learn as much as possible about the next step in your process of becoming an attorney. That step happens to be the admissions process, of which the bar exam is simply a part. If you are about to take the bar exam, you may not want to spend time learning about the process. Too much detail. Yet, it is this level of detail to which you must attend if you are to pass the exam. Therefore, fight the feeling to skip this chapter. Begin focusing on the detail now by taking this opportunity to learn as much about the admissions process for your jurisdiction of choice as you can. Read on.

Getting to Know You

Each state or territory sets its own criteria for admission to practice law within its borders. This is why there are over fifty bar exams and just as many sets of admissions criteria. The admission process can be straightforward or convoluted. It may require evidence of fitness and character to practice, in addition to bar exam passage. It may require an interview, a background check and the like. Familiarize yourself with the admissions process of your chosen jurisdiction.

Criteria for admission to the various jurisdictions can be found in the "Comprehensive Guide to Bar Admissions Requirements," published by the National Conference of Bar Examiners. This guide consists of twelve charts listing admissions criteria for the states and territories, including their bar exam information. You may obtain a free copy from the ABA Order Fulfillment Department, American Bar Association, 750 N. Lake Shore Drive, Chicago, Illinois, 60611, or call the ABA Service Center at (312) 988-5522 for copies. Additional copies are $5.90. Get your copy today and read it.

The Nationals

Almost every jurisdiction has a bar exam, which must be passed as part of its admission criteria. Wisconsin is a notable exception. Wisconsin provides a "diploma privilege." Graduates of the University of Wisconsin and Marquette University law schools need not take and pass the Wisconsin bar exam. All other graduates are faced with the same requirement imposed by the other jurisdictions, that they take and pass the bar exam if they seek admission to the general practice of law.

Before the advent of the *Multistate Bar Examination* (MBE), bar exams tested only the local laws, rules and practices of a given jurisdiction. Knowledge of federal or majority law was therefore unnecessary. The MBE changed all of that. The thinking, which gave rise to the MBE, was that a single standardized exam which tested federal or majority principles, would, in the best case, obviate the need for all or parts of the local exams. Thus, by taking one exam, students would facilitate admission to the differing jurisdictions. In addition, such an exam could ensure a national minimal standard of competency.

This impetus to *nationalize* the bar exam began and continues through the efforts of the National Conference of Bar Examiners or NCBE, the organization which administers the MBE and other "national" exams. The NCBE was established in 1931 as a Section 501(c)(3), not for profit corporation with a stated mission to:

> **Work with other institutions to develop, maintain, and apply reasonable and uniform standards of education and character for eligibility for admission to the practice of law.**

As an affiliated organization of the American Bar Association (ABA), the National Conference of Bar Examiners administers the following exams and programs, in addition to the MBE: The Multistate Professional Responsibility Examination (MPRE); The Multistate Essay Examination (MEE); The Character Report Service (which verifies certain character information); Pre-registration of Law Students; the Cross Reference System (which compiles admission application dates); Score Transfer; and Score Combining. You can obtain more information about these services and the National Conference, itself, by writing to the NCBE, 333 North Michigan Avenue, Suite 1025, Chicago, Illinois 60601-4090, (312) 641-0963.

Notwithstanding the move towards a national bar exam as initiated with the MBE, most jurisdictions still test local law on their own separate bar exam. Now, however, most have added the MBE as a part of that exam. For example, before the MBE, New York's bar exam consisted of twelve (12) essays, 50 multiple choice and 50 short answer questions. When New York adopted the MBE, it eliminated six (6) essays and the 50 short answer questions. Below is a brief synopsis of each of the national exams.

The Multistate Bar Examination (MBE). The MBE is given the last Wednesday in February and July each year. It is a multiple-choice, electronically graded exam. Its 200 questions test six areas of law, Constitutional, Contracts, Criminal, Evidence, Real Property, and Torts. These 200 questions (40 Contracts, 40 Torts, 30 in each of the other areas) are constructed by six committees consisting of law professors, bar examiners and practitioners from across the country. It is considered a "national" exam because it does not test the specifics of local law, instead it relies on fundamental or majority principles of law and the Federal Rules of Evidence. In some jurisdictions, the MBE score is a substantial part of your final exam score. Its importance, therefore, should not be minimized.

Scores are calculated on the number of correct questions, so students are advised to answer all questions. The number answered correctly will constitute the "raw score," which is then converted to a "scale score." Scaling allows the grader to account for the degree of difficulty a particular item represented, when compared to the score students received on that item in prior years. (Hint: obviously, questions must be repeated on subsequent exams; see Chapter Six on repetition.) The scale score is then placed on a "common scale" so that it can be added to the scores received on other portions of the entire exam. It is then "weighted." For example, the MBE's "weight" (or worth) on the New York exam is 40% (the multiple-choice is 15%, and the New York essays are 45%, all equalling 100%).

Since its 1972 inauguration, the Multistate has been adopted by all but four (4) states—Indiana, Iowa, Louisiana and Washington. Certain jurisdictions will accept MBE scores from different jurisdictions: Alabama, Arkansas, Colorado, Connecticut, District of Columbia, Idaho, Illinois, Kansas, Maine, Maryland, Michigan, Minnesota, Mississippi, Missouri, Montana, Nebraska, New Jersey, New York, North Dakota, Utah, Vermont, Virgin Islands, West Virginia, Wisconsin, Wyoming, Guam and the Commonwealth of the Northern Mariana Islands. Others will not. Always check.

You also need to check the jurisdiction to which you seek admission to determine whether it will accept the scores that you received on *earlier* exams and whether the jurisdiction where you sat will transfer scores. Only Alabama, Arizona, California, Colorado, Connecticut, District of Columbia, Florida, Hawaii, Illinois, Kansas, Maryland, Minnesota, Missouri and Virginia so far have authorized the transfer of MBE scores. You must verify any and all transfer arrangements through both boards of bar examiners.

General information on the MBE may be obtained from the National Conference of Bar Examiners, 333 North Michigan Avenue, Chicago, Illinois 60601-4090. You will receive a MBE packet consisting of general information, an application and sample questions and answers. You can order an additional 500 questions and answers without explanations, if you include a check for the $15 fee.

The Multistate Professional Responsibility Examination (MPRE). The
National Conference of Bar Examiners administers the *Multistate Professional
Responsibility Examination (MPRE)*. Its purpose is to test an applicant's knowl-
edge of ethics. This exam, which can be taken before graduation (except in
Florida, which requires that it be taken after graduation), is also national in that
it does not test local rules. It requires knowledge of the ABA Code of Profes-
sional Responsibility, the Model Rules of Professional Conduct and the ABA
Code of Judicial Conduct. Copies of these items can be obtained from the ABA,
Attn: Service Department, P.O. Box 1090-82, Chicago, Illinois, 60611-9082,
(312) 988-5855.

The MPRE is a two hour exam which consists of 50 multiple choice questions. It is now required in 40 jurisdictions. MPRE scoring mirrors the MBE.
The number of correct answers constitutes the raw score which is then scaled.
Each state determines its own passing score. The range of scores tends to be
between 72 and 85. Nevada, Arizona, Colorado, Idaho, Minnesota, Oregon
and Texas have highs of 85. New York has a low of 72.

To obtain information about the MPRE, contact the National Conference
of Bar Examiners, MPRE Application Department, P.O. Box 4001, Iowa City,
Iowa 52243, (319) 337-1287.

The Multistate Essay Examination (MEE). In an effort to standardize
the essay portion of the bar exam, the National Conference designed the
Multistate Essay Examination (MEE). The MEE consists of six questions covering Agency & Partnerships, Commercial Paper, Conflicts, Corporations, Family Law, Federal Civil Procedure, Sales, Secured Transactions, Trusts & Estates and Future Interests. This three hour exam tests four skills: the ability to
discern legal issues; the ability to separate relevant from non-relevant facts and
issues; legal reasoning, and legal knowledge. Although the MEE is still experi-
mental, students have sat for it in Arkansas, D.C., Idaho, Illinois, Kansas, New
Mexico, Utah and West Virginia, as part of their bar exams.

You can obtain an information booklet containing sample questions and
answers by writing to the NCBE, 333 North Michigan Avenue, Suite 1025,Chi-
cago, Illinois, 60601-4090, (312) 641-0963. To find out whether your jurisdiction requires the MEE, contact the bar examiners in the state where you
plan to take the exam. Given the variability of bar exams, this advice should be
followed on any aspect of the bar exam. You should obtain as much informa-

tion as you can on the exam you are planning to take so that you can direct your energies appropriately.

The Locals

It will be a while, if at all, before the MEE or some other standardized essay exam gains acceptance to the point of eliminating the local law part of bar exams. So until that time, you should gain a firm understanding of the processes and peculiarities of your jurisdiction's exam and its administration.

Each jurisdiction has a committee, board or office which prepares and administers the bar exam. In New York, it is the New York State Board of Law Examiners. This entity oversees the admissions process, prepares and administers the New York exam on behalf of the New York State Court of Appeals. In California, it is the Office of Admissions, the State Bar of California. Write to your board of bar examiners, requesting any and all information about the bar exam and the admissions process. You can find out the exact name of the local board and its address by using the "Comprehensive Guide to Bar Admissions," discussed earlier in this chapter. In the alternative, you can refer to *Appendix B* in this book. That *Appendix* contains contact information for the boards, along with a description of information they will send. For example, the Florida Board will send you the rules governing the admissions process. These rules detail the application process and describe the exam. You should obtain and read all the information available about your exam well before you begin studying for it. You need to do this to know about the mechanics of applying for the exam as much as you need to know the art of studying for the exam.

The Process Begins

Some law schools will obtain bar exam applications for their students. Some do not. Always check with your school's Registrar. Once you receive the application packet, read it carefully. Do not depend on word of mouth for information. You need first-hand information on what you need to do and by when. For example, you may need to be fingerprinted or photographed. You may need to supply handwriting samples. You may need certified checks or money orders. All deadlines for any such submissions should be circled in red on your monthly calendars discussed in Chapter Four, listing what must be done and by when. The process can get rather complicated, so the better acquainted you are with it, the easier time you'll have completing it. Take New York, for example.

The application packet is mailed *gratis* (for now). The completed application must be accompanied by a $250 money order or cashier's check. Applications with personal checks will be rejected and returned. In some instances, there is a fee just for the application packet, e.g., Kentucky, Colorado, and Idaho charge $10 for their packets. Telephone the jurisdiction first to find out about fees for the application. Of course, this fee will be separate from the filing or exam fee which must accompany the completed application. Those fees range from $200 to $1100. Start saving money now if you anticipate financial constraints.

Read all instructions before completing the application. Consider photocopying the original and using the copy as a draft. Once completed, note *when* to mail the application. For example, the New York Board of Law Examiners must receive your completed application (which should be mailed return receipt requested) post marked at least 60 days, but not more than 90 days before the date of the exam which you intend to take. You will need to be vigilant during your study period to ensure that you receive your letter of admission and your assignment to a test center in advance of the exam. Make sure that you have a copy of your completed application, just in case. You may receive a receipt for your application. See sample A below. Safeguard the receipt, along with a copy of your certified check, again, just in case.

A.
*(These samples are presented for form only. Rely only
on the actual documents received.)*

STATE BOARD OF LAW EXAMINERS

Dear Candidate:
    We acknowledge receipt of your application for admission to the Bar examination. Please note that the number appearing in the upper left hand corner near your address is your permanent file number. You should refer to it in all future correspondence with the Board to expedite processing of your communication.
    Your application will be processed and if it is complete, an admission pass to the examination will be mailed to you. You should receive this pass about one

week before the examination. . . .

Sincerely,

Executive Secretary

If your admission ticket does not come on time, do not panic. Call the bar administrators to make sure that it is *en route*, so that you do not waste time or energy on a potential distraction. If you cannot get through to them and you are enrolled in a bar review course, call and enlist their assistance. Once it is in hand, read the admission ticket. It should designate location, times and seat number. See sample B below.

B.

(These samples are presented for form only. Rely only on the actual documents received.)

STATE BOARD OF LAW EXAMINERS

This is your admission ticket to take the bar examination at the following time and place:

PASSENGER SHIP TERMINAL
YOUR SEAT NUMBER IS <u>1883</u>
TUES., FEB. 21 -- 8:45 A.M. to 12:15 P.M. and 1:30 P.M. to 4:45 P.M.
    LOCAL SECTION
WED., FEB. 22 -- 8:45 A.M. to 12 NOON and 1:30 P.M. to 4:30 P.M.
    MULTISTATE SECTION

FOOD, DRINK, BAGS, BOOKS, BACKPACKS, ETC. ARE NOT PERMITTED AT YOUR SEAT. THERE ARE NO FACILITIES AVAILABLE TO STORE YOUR BELONGINGS. THEY MUST BE PLACED, <u>AT YOUR OWN RISK</u>, IN DESIGNATED AREAS AT THE EXAMINATION CENTERS.

The examination will start at 9:00 a.m., but you should be in your seat by 8:45 a.m., in order to read the instructions to be found there. You should also listen attentively to the oral instructions which will be given between 8:50 and 9:00 a.m.

> You are responsible for providing your own pens and
> no. 2 pencils.

Pay attention to the location. If you do not know where it is, go there at least once before the exam to work out travel arrangements and to get a sense of the space where you will be sitting. Notice on our sample above that the candidate was assigned to a passenger ship terminal. You would want to visit such a unique location in advance of the exam to determine whether there are characteristics of the test site that may impair your ability to concentrate and, if necessary, to prepare for them. For example, bring ear plugs if it is noisy or carry a sweater for drafts. You may need to bring to the attention of those in authority such potential distractions as allergens, physical obstructions or inaccessibility of facilities.

Local Law Day

Most bar exams are given over a two-day period. One day of the bar exam is devoted solely to the MBE. The other day(s) is considered the local day where a jurisdiction tests its local rules and practice. The format is generally essay. Notable exceptions are California and Hawaii, which administer three day exams. The local law tested by many of the jurisdictions usually consists of the local practice rules and procedures, the domestic relations law of the locale, the law of decedents' estates, local criminal law and procedure, real estate law, corporate or business law. The number of legal subject areas tested depends upon the state and may vary greatly. Florida usually tests eleven (11) subjects. New Jersey tests on six (6) subjects but you need familiarity with a handful of others. Delaware tests on fourteen (14). New York probably wins the prize for testing on more than twenty (20).

The format of the question also depends on the individual state. New York asks essay and multiple-choice questions. Some jurisdictions are following California's lead by adopting "performance" questions. The goal of performance exams is to evaluate an applicant's ability to digest and analyze facts, and to apply law in client-based settings. To this end, the performance question provides students with the necessary documents, usually contained in a "file" and "library." The files provide the facts of a given case and the libraries contain relevant case law and statutes. Using the two, the applicant is asked to draft a memorandum, brief, letter, or other legal documents, setting forth his/ her analysis of the issues identified. The questions are graded based on responsiveness, thoroughness, organization and accuracy. Students in Georgia, Virginia and New Mexico have been given the option of taking a half-day performance exam, administered by the National Conference.

California provides copies of sample performance exams. If you are taking the California bar exam, you should receive an order form along with your application. For an $8.00 fee, you can obtain performance questions. For another $5.00, you can get essay questions and answers. Write to: The Committee of Bar Examiners of the State Bar of California, Office of Admissions, 555 Franklin Street, San Francisco, California 94102, (415) 561-8303 or 1149 South Hill Street, 10th Floor, Los Angeles, California 90015, (213) 580-5500.

The National Conference of Bar Examiners will also provide you with a sample performance test and answer. If you receive their 1990 sample test, you should note that it is based upon a California test administered in July of 1987. Its time allotments may be different from other performance exams. Take that into account before you practice it at home. You can obtain a copy of the sample exam by writing: NCBE, 333 North Michigan Avenue, Suite 1025, Chicago, Illinois 60601-4090, (312) 641-0963.

"65.000 or Bust"

There are different types of scores which you can receive on the local portion of the bar exam, each corresponding to one of the separate sections. The sections are often of unequal weight, requiring the use of measures to provide an overall passing score; hence, the scaled and/or combined scores. Where available, learn the total score you need to pass the exam. For example, Oklahoma's passing score is 2400. Pennsylvania has a score of 129. In Colorado, it is 276. In Texas, it is 675. Oregon's is 65.000. This information is generally contained in the information packet mailed to candidates by the local boards of bar examiners. You can also find it in the National Conference's Guide. *Appendix B* also provides this data.

Knowing this information allows you to visualize a passing score. Once you have put form to an idea, it will make it easier to attain because you can actually *see* your goal. There is less mystery, more certainty. From here until the exam is over, your lucky number should be the score needed to pass your bar exam. Once you have fixed the passing score in your head, visualize that score on bar-related documents you may encounter. See it on any sample bar exams or questions you may take. Obtaining such materials can be as simple as contacting the bar examiners. For example, New York sends a sample bar exam as part of its information packet. Vermont will send prior essay questions with its application packet. For a nominal fee, you may obtain sample questions, if not full exams, from such jurisdictions as:

> *California*: $5.00 for essay questions and selected answers. $8.00 for performance tests and selected answers.

> *Colorado*: $3.00 for essay questions asked on a recent bar exam. $3.00 for exam and discussions of questions asked on a recent bar exam. $3.00 for a score sheet for questions asked on a recent bar exam.

> *Connecticut*: $15 for a copy of prior exam questions. $25 for a copy of prior exam answers (includes questions).

> *Florida*: $20 for a copy of essay-type questions which appeared on a previously administered General Bar Examination.

> *Montana*: For the cost of duplication, examples of past essay questions are made available.

> *Ohio*: Publishes essay questions and a selection of passing answers shortly after the announcement of exam results.

> *Puerto Rico*: Publishes a handbook with sample multiple choice questions and answers from preceding bar examinations.

Some states send prior questions as part of their application packets which require the payment of a fee. Check your jurisdiction. See *Appendix B*.

*   *   *

With these materials in hand, a quick, initial read through will show you that it's not as bad as you thought. Indeed, it is quite *do-able*. Maybe you'll be one of the students to believe me when I say that the bar exam will be one of the easier exams you will ever take *and pass*. Therefore, visualize that passing score on your exam booklet. Write that score down on post-its and put them on your refrigerator door and on the bathroom mirror. When defeatist thoughts or contrary people come your way, see your passing score, your name in print *and force yourself back into a "Yes I Can" mode.*

CHAPTER THREE

DISCIPLINE THYSELF

I give a bar exam lecture on *organization*. My thesis is that if you organize your life and study routine, a well organized exam approach and answer will follow. I developed this topic after years of noting the differences between those students who passed and those who didn't. A key difference is *discipline*. Students who passed exhibited the necessary *discipline* to order their priorities and organize their lives around meeting those priorities. Their discipline extended to the design, implementation and maintenance of a study regimen. *Discipline,* therefore, is the second part of **The Program**. Once you have adopted the *Yes I Can* attitude, you must discipline yourself to identify and plan for all the things that you can and must do to pass the bar.

Expect the Unexpected

You can encounter the unexpected at any time. You walk outside to find your car being towed. Your first cousin on your mother's side was arrested last night for armed robbery. A desirable though unexpected event can be as potentially disruptive as a undesirable one. After years of trying, you have just learned that you are pregnant. While you may not be able to control the occurrence or the consequences of the unexpected event, especially a traumatic one, you may be able to manage your reaction to it. One aspect of the bar exam preparation period is *a plan to avoid crises*. After helping hundreds of students prepare for the exam, I have identified certain predictable crises that may disrupt your work. I list here those crises and suggested plans of avoidance.

Your finances. Own up to your debts and face-off with the "collectors." Do not ignore them, otherwise they will act up when it is least advantageous to you, the Tuesday before the Wednesday MBE. Many creditors may be sympathetic to a bar candidate's request for forbearance while you struggle to become a more *economically* viable member of society. Work out a payment plan in advance of the preparation period to commence after the exam. If the matter has to go to court, get there sooner rather than later. *Judges had to take the bar exam, too.*

My Cousin Vinny. You are a lawyer because you have a law degree. You are not an attorney because you have yet to be admitted to practice. If Cousin Vinny or Brother Leroy is arrested, you can give your family the name and telephone number of a good private attorney, the Office of the Public Defender, or the Legal Aid Society. You can stop by the home to give comfort. You do not, however, wait hours at Central Booking or Arraignments to talk to Vinny or Leroy. Even if you had the time (which you do not), you should not because you are not his attorney and there is no *client/cousin* privilege.

A wedding in the family. If it is your wedding, wait until the exam is well over. Even if there is a fair amount of pressure being put on you to have the wedding during the time you are studying for the bar exam, resist it. The wedding plans will inevitably eat into your study plans.

If you are a bridesmaid or groomsman in someone else's wedding, make your apologies up front for being generally unavailable, and then ask the happy couple to schedule events as convenient to your schedule as possible. If they cannot or will not, beg off and give a nice gift.

Illness. Make sure that in responding to this event you distinguish what you *can* do from what you want to do or think you should do. With the exception of a hospitalized child or other relative, you may be able to work your study schedule around visiting hours. It may sound weird, but having to study for the exam during an illness of a loved one may turn out to be a blessing. Work is good therapy; so is study. The exam may give you the structure needed to amass the strength to see your loved one to health and yourself through the exam.

The "I've been meaning to's." If you have been meaning to get a fire extinguisher for your home, do it. If you have been meaning to get the car fixed, do it. If you have been meaning to get that mammogram, do it. *Do it*, before *it* does you.

Early in your preparation period, give yourself a *Junk Week*, a time to do all things most likely to lurk in the background waiting to trip you up. Make a list of all these things, the longer the better. Then go down the list. In my case, there is a special method to this madness. I make sure to hit my favorite stores. I spend at least an hour in each one of them, rolling an enormous shopping cart up and down every aisle. I look at almost everything stocked in office supplies, and in drug and household supplies. I spend about $75 and come home with a three-month supply of ziploc bags, Tylenol, vitamins, dental floss, three-ring binders, legal pads, pens and pencils, paper clips and at least a gallon of laundry detergent. This is my way of tricking myself into thinking that I am safe from all easily avoidable minor crises. The trick often works, leaving me with only those not-so minor crises that will happen no matter how well I prepare.

There are some events, like the unexpected death of a loved one, a serious fire, the birth of children, that may so profoundly influence you that you may not be able or desire to return to equilibrium to meet the challenge of the bar exam. You must judge your abilities in the face of these events and decide whether it may be better to deal with the bar exam at another time, if ever (and that's o.k., too).

Expect the Expected

Other priorities will compete for our time and attention during this period. There may be *significant others*, adults and children, full-time or part-time work, community, political or religious activities. Some of these activities can be put on hold during your study period, others cannot. Here are some ways to ensure that the bar exam priority remains one of your main priorities.

Relationships. Some view familial relationships as hindrances during this time. Relatives make demands on your time and whatever little money you may have. Children recognize only their needs. *Significant others* seem to be jealous of the time you spend away from them. When these demands seem most oppressive, you should take a moment to look at it *their* way.

For the last three or so years, you have been *away* from them, if not physically then mentally, as you worked to complete law school. You made new friends and were involved in new experiences not often shared by loved ones. In many ways, you have gone through a subtle change in the way you speak, think, even look. Although they could not be prouder of their *lawyer*, they have missed you and want to be with you. Although they may seem demanding now, they have usually been there for you. They have loved you, guided you, prayed for you (like my brother *Marvin*), supported you, and given you money. While you might not have recognized it as such, they have also given you structure and a tangible reason for passing. Consider yourself, therefore, *advantaged* in having these relationships. Cultivate them, especially during this period. Here are ways.

1. Set weekly times during which you give them your undivided attention. Explain *their time* in the context of your other competing priorities. This affirms their value to you while informing them of your need to attend to the other priority of passing the bar exam.

2. Tell them exactly what you are going through. Let them hear a bar review tape or come to a lecture so that they can appreciate the magnitude of this challenge. You will probably only have to do this once. Make sure they have something to do to occupy themselves while you are away studying.

3. Give yourself over to them for one or two full days during this period. Let them plan for it, look forward to it, exhaust themselves during it and leave you alone after it.

4. If all else fails, ask them, *"How many times do you want me to go through this?"*

Work (as in, for a living). If at all possible, do *not!* If you need to work to eat, to support self and others, then you must. If you are working long hours to support a grand lifestyle, you must decide whether the bar exam is your priority. There is so much to learn during this period that you need all possible additional hours for study.

If you do work, turn that into an advantage, too. You need not worry about getting a job after the exam. You may not need to interrupt your study routine to interview or to distribute resumés. You probably have a ready-made schedule to work around. To keep the bar a priority, adopt similar strategies as those used in your personal relationships:

1. Talk to your colleagues and supervisors. Make them a part of the process. Assure them that you will get your job done, but that you are on a tight schedule from which you do not want to deviate. Use your commute, your breaks and lunch times to study.

2. Save up your vacation time so that you can take it all at once, usually towards the end of the study period as bar review courses and your own schedule will require more flexibility and time.

3. If your colleagues are not collegial about your bar
    preparation, at least you will know that. The key is to
    bring it all into the open if possible. You should not
    expend energy keeping your preparation for the exam
    a secret.

Community/religious/political. Some things have to give. You may have
an untapped reservoir of surplus energy, but it is not inexhaustible. If you must
involve yourself in these activities during this period, again, explain the other
pulls on your time to those involved. Ask for diminished involvement with the
promise of greater participation after the exam. Note that I differentiate between religious (church, temple, mosque-related) and spiritual activities. Post-
pone the former, protect the latter. Nurture your spirit, especially now.

Me, Myself and I. You must also manage yourself:

> *A sound mind in a sound body.* Exercise regularly;
> eat regularly; get enough sleep.
> *Listen to your body.* From little aches do big pains
> grow. Get a physical. Check out that ache. Get your
> teeth fixed. Anticipate your reaction to stress and mini-
> mize its disruptive capacity; keep two pairs of glasses,
> dentures, etc.
> *Don't judge a book by its cover.* Get a hair style that
> will last with the least amount of grooming, e.g., braids;
> trim nails and use clear nail polish (if you must); adopt
> a low maintenance uniform, e.g., baggy jeans and tee
> shirts.

*   *   *

A *Yes I Can* attitude without discipline is like one hand clapping. It does
not work. Discipline allows you to balance priorities and to maintain that balance, especially when challenged. During the weeks before the exam, you
may experience severe mood swings. There is the potential for feeling incred-
ible elation one minute (possibly because of graduation), and devastating anxi-

ety the next, probably caused by the fast approaching bar exam.   If we learn to manage that which we can, life's crises or unexpected events may not be so disruptive of our plans that we are unable to recover our balance. *Keep to The Program to keep your balance.*

CHAPTER FOUR

KEEP TIME ON YOUR SIDE

"I can't." Maybe this is your first response to the idea of learning multiple areas of law, listening to hundreds of lecture hours, answering thousands of MBE questions, working at a full-time job, taking care of a family and job-hunting, all in ten to twelve weeks. Even if you don't actually say the words, you may act them out just the same.

You may begin with missing a lecture (for no *good* reason) and falling behind. Then you may lose a night or two of sleep and suddenly begin feeling queasy. A day or two or three will pass and you will look up, see how much time you have lost and start struggling to catch up. Before you know it, you will start feeling overwhelmed. You will begin arguing with your mate, kicking your dog and yelling at the kids. Worse yet, you will look for *excuses* for not studying, which excuses (I might add) will become your reasons for failing. *You had to work. The exam is biased. The review course "sucked."*

The best way for you to beat this scenario? Don't start it! You do that by hauling out those very hopes, ideas, dreams and wishes which brought you to this point in becoming a lawyer. You restart your *Yes I Can* attitude, and you summon up the discipline demanded by **The Program** to make those dreams happen. That discipline, in this context, keeps you from thinking of the exam process as a monolith, like some huge, one-dimensional obstacle that you cannot see over, under or around. Any person in his or her right mind will surely become overwhelmed at the thought of doing all that has to be done to prepare for the bar exam in what seems to be such a ridiculously short a period of time. By sticking to **The Program**, each time the *"I can't"* thought seeks to surface and the panic seeks expression, visualize the explosion of that monolith and see its much smaller (and infinitely more manageable) pieces hit the ground. With each piece representing an aspect of the preparation process which you must complete, see yourself picking the pieces up, one at a time. Now you can examine each piece, determine its place in your schedule and design a plan on when and how you will address it.

Gladys F.

Gladys is an articulate and bright woman. She had such an easy-going personality that we became fast friends from the first tutoring session. After two surprisingly un-productive sessions which showed a lack of discipline on her part, I confronted Gladys with my suspicions that she was not putting in the required amount of study time. She confessed to me that a friend of hers once told her that she shouldn't take the bar exam right after gradua-tion because she would be too excited to concentrate well enough to study. Since her friend was one she respected (and who failed the exam on his first try right after law school graduation), she gave his words some credence.

In reaction to this "advice," I asked Gladys to keep a diary, listing all of her activities hourly until our next meeting. Upon our review of her diary, which looked more like the "Arts & Leisure" section of the newspaper than the schedule of someone about to take the bar exam in eight weeks, Gladys realized that if she failed the exam it would not be because she was "high" on graduation. It would be because she was not working, not putting in the time.

You are going to receive more advice about passing the bar than you thought possible. Everyone has an approach, a theory, a story. Use your common sense to filter the information given. If you want to take it right after law school, do it. If you paid your money for advice (a bar review course, an essay workshop, *this book*), listen to those who have devoted much of their time and attention to other people's passing of the exam, not just their own. Ignore the amateurs. Follow a "pro's" advice.

Once we placed Gladys' advice in context, we were able to redirect the energy she had invested in thinking she would not pass and put into action a plan designed to assist her to pass the bar. Gladys and I looked at the actual time she had to prepare for the exam. We made lists and schedules. We worked at calendars. We started by listing the things she had to do in the weeks to come:

- study for exam
- take sample bar exam (2 days)
- be in sister's wedding
- get application in
- attend bar review course
- religious observance
- family

As Gladys was scheduled to take the July bar exam, we began planning her preparation and study time to commence during the month of May. Using the schedule of her bar review course, we noted the daily subjects to be covered. We then added family responsibilities, e.g., her sister's wedding. We noted bar-related activities, e.g., application deadlines, lecture dates, and Multistate workshops, and we listed personal matters, like paying bills. See *Appendix C* for sample schedule.

With these monthly planners, Gladys was able to see clearly how much time she had before the exam and how she intended to use that time. Moreover, we were able to determine how she actually used that time, as well as to update her monthly plans as the unexpected, and not so unexpected came up.

You should engage in the same type of scheduling. Using the blank calendars in *Appendix D*, you can put in all the activities that you already know of starting in May. If you are planning to take the February bar, begin in December. Even if you are not taking a review course, you can still use a copy of their schedule as a guide. Write to them asking for a packet of information for their course. A schedule should be included. If not, get one from a friend. Now, do exactly as Gladys did, so that you have completed May, June and July calendars (December, January and February calendars for the winter exam).

This type of visual, objective, goal-oriented planning will compel you to look at the entire picture of subject mastery and priority balancing, without the overload mentioned earlier because, this time, you are not looking at these priorities in the abstract as one giant task. You are visualizing them individually, planning them in detail, and thereby making them manageable.

Every Minute Counts

Monthly planning is only half the battle. You must also schedule your daily activities, hour by hour. If you do not, you may find yourself with "the best laid plans" and no time in which to complete them.

Chelsea C.

Chelsea is a divorced mother of three. She always seems positive about life, so it did not take her much time to adopt the necessary attitude about the bar exam and preparation for it. Law was a second career for her. She had taught elementary school for twenty years. She was no stranger to hard work and was focused on becoming an attorney.

Chelsea knew how to study. As she began to do so one morning, she decided to catch-up with her reading (50 pages); take a practice exam to mail-in; and read and outline oil and gas law all before her family awakened.

After three hours, however, when she heard the first stirring of her children, she had only completed her reading assignment. As she prepared to begin the practice exam, she heard the faucet dripping. The sound was so annoying that she stopped doing questions to try and fix it herself. That took 15 minutes. Since she was already up, she figured she would call her sister to find out when they were going shopping for dresses for their daughters for their piano recital that night. That took another 45 minutes. Finally her "friend" called to see how her studies were going. That call conjured up a most pleasant fantasy which Chelsea could not resist.

All told, she spent an hour and a half on matters other than her studies. She thought about her friend, and then about this feeling she had been sensing in her stomach which she keep meaning to go to the doctor about. She eventually got around to thinking about death and dying by the time she looked up to see her sleepy-eyed, two-year old walking towards "Mommy."

Chelsea's plan for the morning was too ambitious for the time allotted. She could not do all that she had wanted to do in just three hours. She might have realized that subconsciously and that awareness gave her an excuse for not completing the day's task. Even if she had chosen a more limited goal, she had not planned the rest of her day sufficiently to avoid worry about other priorities while she studied. She had not paid attention to her "bodily signals" so as to prevent them (or the consequence thereof) from becoming a source of concern. And she had not sufficiently detailed what she intended to study.

In order to focus, you must schedule every minute of every day between now and the bar exam. Had Chelsea scheduled her day accordingly, the choices for her would have been clearer: *worry about death and dying or study.* Your choices can be made just as clear, if you schedule your days in detail.

Begin with a list of all the activities you must accomplish on any given day. These activities tend to be recurring. A typical list may include some of the following:

- *prepare for bar review class*
- *review notes from last lecture*
- *take an essay question*
- *do 50 multiple choice or multistate questions*
- *finish bar exam application*
- *pay bills*
- *eat*
- *spend time with family/friends*
- *work*

With your basic schedule already filled in on your charts, you can now add today's priorities: what you will do and when. Schedule the most difficult task for that time of day when you are most alert. Some people are most alert during the morning hours; others at night. You probably have a good idea of your biorhythm. Use it. Also, use your awareness of your own natural time-blocks, when you need to stretch, take a walk, clear your head, to schedule your breaks. Put in the time you need to switch gears, be it every 45, 60 or 90 minutes, and how long a break you need before you can settle back to work.

Accordingly, the daily schedule for a morning person, who is not working, could look like this:

5:30 a.m. - 7:30	-	exercise, breakfast, spend time with family
7:30 - 8:00	-	break
8:00 - 9:00	-	review notes of lecture from day before
9:00 - 9:50	-	take practice essay questions in the same subject reviewed in yesterday's lecture
9:50 - 10:30	-	review essay, sample answer and notes to identify problem areas (keep a list of same)
10:30 - 10:45	-	break

10:45-11:30	-	take 25 multistate questions in the same area as lecture and essay, identify problems
11:30 - 1:00 p.m	-	review incorrect responses; check to see if same issues from essay were troublesome on MBE
1:00 - 2:00	-	lunch, watch TV, play or engage in some other mindless activity
2:00 - 4:00	-	read materials for today's lecture
4:00 - 6:00	-	travel to lecture, (do multiple choice en route) purchase supper to eat during lecture
6:00 - 10:00	-	bar review lecture
10:00 p.m.	-	travel home, see your name in print, go to sleep

A schedule for someone who works at night and who chooses not to take a bar review course might look like this:

midnight - 8:00 am	-	work
(1 hour lunch)	-	do 25 multistate for 45 minutes and review 15 minutes
(15 min breaks)	-	multiple choice questions
8:00 am - 9:00 am	-	travel home, see your name in print, listen to tape or do multiple choice (if not driving)
9:00 am - 4:00 p.m.	-	sleep
4:00 - 7:00	-	listen to tapes
7:00 - 8:00	-	dinner, interact with family, exercise
8:00 - 8:50	-	do practice essay exam
8:50 - 9:00	-	review sample answer and notes
9:00 - 9:45	-	do 25 MBE
9:45 - 11:00	-	review MBE answers
11:00 - 12 mid.	-	travel, listen to tape or do multiple choice

There are only two scheduled days off—Memorial day and July 4th, if you are taking the July bar exam. If you are taking the February bar then take off the first night of Hanukkah or Christmas and New Year's day. All other days, weekends and holidays are scheduled for study, even if, in the case of a sabbath or holiday, you can work only before or after sundown. Those days might look like this:

Day One -   *9:00 - 12:00; 1:30 - 4:30*
                    catch up time to make up for slippage.

Day Two -   *9:00 - 12:00;* 1:30 - 3:30
                    review problem areas and
                    do essays/MBE in those areas

The schedules presented here are those of actual students, who passed on the first try. They worked because they were tailored to meet the needs of the individual. Your schedule must be similarly tailored. When carefully structured, it will provide you with enough time, no matter what other competing priorities exist. The challenge for you is to devise your own schedule and to make it work. The discipline that you have been developing to ensure a positive attitude, and in maintaining your relationships is what you need most now in your scheduling.

*   *   *

A final point. Slippage happens. Don't panic. You can catch up if you find the source of it. Are you feeling overwhelmed despite **The Program**? Not to worry. See the *explosion* and pick up one piece at a time. Are you losing or giving up control of your time? Take it back; get lost (go somewhere where *they* cannot find you). Are the review courses scheduling more lectures? Extend your study hours during the day and/or night (whichever one fits your rhythm). Do you feel like you are back in first year law school, starting over again just when you felt you had earned the right to coast? Get over it.

Whatever the reason for the slippage, stop it as soon as you can. It is never too late. Just as you can drift into feeling overwhelmed, you can work yourself back into feeling in charge again. *Visualize, chant "Yes I Can", and go back to your plan and stick to it.*

CHAPTER FIVE

A TIME TO STUDY

There was a student at my *alma mater*, who was notorious for sitting in the lunchroom all day, playing bridge. He would also sit all evening in the pub, playing bridge. And he would play bridge all weekend in the student lounge. No one recalls ever seeing him in class, but we all remember that he "aced" exams and made law review. Everyone knows a student like that. Now is the time to forget about 'em!

Some people can pass exams with minimal study, especially when the exam involves a single subject area. Few people can cram for the bar exam *and pass it*. There is too much information to absorb in too little time. Most people must utilize a planned study procedure for the bar exam because of the amount of information to learn and retain, and because of the uniqueness of the exam itself (consisting, as it does, of structurally different components, covering multiple subjects and lasting anywhere from two to four days). The task of learning so much so quickly, and the importance of passing makes a successful study strategy a must.

In the preceding chapters, we have been changing the way you view the bar exam and how you mentally prepare for it. You are now ready for a method by which you must *physically* study for it. Having created the most exquisite schedules, you may think that you are ready to get to work. Think, again. There are certain basic principles to understand before you begin.

Quality Time and Space

When is the best time of day for you to study? Where? How long does that time last and what follows it? Consider Sean's story.

Sean X.

Sean is a management consultant, who tells a story of a corporate CEO with whom he regularly met. This CEO, according to Sean, would eventually rise from his chair during the course of a meeting, shake Sean's hand and politely dismiss him. After this happened several times, Sean finally asked the CEO how he knew when it

*was time to quit without looking at his watch. "Simple,"
the CEO is alleged to have told him. "I know I have a
90-minute attention span. When my mind starts to wan-
der, I know your time is up."*

Knowing your attention span is as important and basic as knowing your telephone number, social security number or ATM PIN number. Once you know how much time you can sit still and concentrate on a matter, you can work within it or stretch it. Similarly, knowing the best, worst and middling times for you, through each day, and building these time-blocks into your sched-ule—fitting the hardest, easiest and most routine tasks into the times where they fit best—is a key part of any successful plan. If you need more study time, extend your day by starting earlier or ending later. But know where your qual-ity work time naturally falls and how long it is. That is the time for your most important, difficult and rewarding work. Guard those time blocks as if they were gold, and let the rest of your day fall into place around them.

In addition to knowing your quality time, you must also create a physical space which helps you to concentrate. Some people study best in solitude. Some people study best with music. You must determine, based upon what you now know of the exam and yourself, what will work best for you. You may need to create quality space, a place of your own, your office of the moment, your bar exam study corner. Create such space at home and away from home and protect it against interruptions. For instance,

    Eliminate telephone interruptions. Switch on your an-
swering machine. (Buy one now if you don't already have
one). Ask yourself, "what emergency will arise in three hours
that will require my attention?" Unless you are also a surgeon
with a skill few others have; or need to obtain a stay of execu-
tion for a client on "Death Row", the answer is "few."

    Pre-arrange reliable child care. Have your providers lined
up. Place their names and telephone numbers on your schedule. Make sure your provider has your household list of emergency telephone numbers and knows where you are. Promise
children some time together for an adventure after you have
finished the day's study.

    Study in a library. If you do not have "quality space" at home, use a public library. For a small fee, you may be able to use the library of a nearby law school. Check with your bar review course, with lawyers, or bar associations for quality space locations.

Study Groups

Study groups tend to proliferate in law school. A variation of that model, which is more suitable for bar exam preparation, is a "study buddy." Find one or two people who you like, trust, respect and arrange to study with them once a week. These buddies are valuable resources. If you have difficulty understanding a lecturer, others can fill in the blanks. If a class is missed, you can borrow a member's notes. But don't abuse it. This is not college!

Use each other to tackle problems, work out uncertainties, share apprehensions and provide aid and comfort. You and your study buddy should separately complete essay questions under simulated conditions (that means timing yourselves) and then objectively review, assess and comment on each other's answers. Listen and incorporate the feedback. It can improve your answers.

Helpful Study Hints

Study in 3 hour blocks. The individual session of most bar exams takes around three hours. Each of your study sessions should be as long as an exam session so that you get used to concentrating for that length of time. Don't set up distractions. Have everything you need at hand before you start work; books, old exams, pads, pencils, pens, coffee.

Take notes. Buy the lined paper used in law school. You remember it. The margin is almost in the middle of the page. To the right of the margin, make notes of materials read; to the left write lecture notes. See *Appendix E* for samples.

Concentrate. Concentrate on what you are reading. If our mind wanders, get up, stretch, walk around, sit back down, then return to work by rereading the material you just glossed over.

Repeat. Read and take notes on the materials for the day's lecture. Listen to the lecture. Take notes. Answer an essay question on the same subject matter. Reread your answer. Compare it to the sample answer. Take an MBE/multiple choice test on the same topic. Review the topic. Do an outline.

Outline. It's much better to *learn* the materials, where possible. The extent to which you make this information a part of your permanent knowledge, the easier it will be to recall it. An outline contains your understanding of an area of the law. After reviewing an area, Labor Law, for example, it is best to close your books and write down everything you know about the subject, then return to the books to fill in missing information. See *Appendix F* for an example.

*   *   *

When I think back on my own bar preparation strategy, it seems surprisingly simple. I awoke every morning at 5:00 a.m. I'm a morning person. I would jog to the tennis courts and practice against a wall for 30 minutes. I would jog back by 6:00, at which time my family would be up and getting ready for work. I would interact with them until they left by 8:20. By 9:00, I was ready to review my notes of the lecture from the night before. From 9:00-9:50, I would take a practice essay question in that subject area and review my answer using the model until 10:00. From 10:00-12 noon, I would review that subject area. From 12:00-1:00 p.m., I would eat lunch, watch T.V. and make or receive telephone calls (I told friends and family to call during this hour). From 1:00-3:00 p.m., I read and made notes from the materials to be covered in that evening's lecture. I would then get ready to take the 4:20 bus to the train and would do multiple-choice questions en route. After I'd order my pumpernickel bagel with cream cheese, and extra light coffee, I'd take my seat (in the rear left of the hall), usually with my study buddy, Wes S., for the 6 o'clock lecture. Travelling home at 11:00 p.m. allowed me time to think about the trip I had planned to take after the exam and the great cases I would litigate once admitted. Saturdays were my days for slippage and family matters. I was, after all, the maid of honor in my sister's upcoming wedding. I'd go to church on Sundays and then meet Wes to take practice exam questions, review each other's work and then goof-off.

Simplicity is the key to a successful study regimen. ***Keep it simple. Keep it tight. And above all, keep to it.***

CHAPTER SIX

EXAM DAY

The discipline you have been developing in shifting your mindset about the bar exam, organizing your life, planning and scheduling your activities, and creating a study routine, is the same discipline that you will bring to the exam itself. But before you open an exam booklet, you will have to call upon that discipline to help you overcome another challenge.

Exam Anxiety

In theater, it is called "stage fright." Opening Night is approaching and you panic. You can't force yourself to go on stage. You can't remember your lines. You just want to go home. That kind of fear can cause similar behavior the closer you get to exam day. You tire easily but can't sleep. Your appetite is gone or you sleep and eat too much. You easily lose your concentration. You can't remember legal principles. You just want to stay in bed.

While a little anxiety is not a bad thing in that it helps to keep you working and motivated, too much may cause you to shut down. To keep this from happening, find your balance again.

Know Yourself. You are no stranger to anxiety. Having made it through school, by the time you begin the preparation period for the bar exam, you will have experienced exam anxiety enough times in your life to anticipate it. Use that knowledge to meet the anxiety and to dispel it. If you tend to react physically to stress, prepare yourself for it well before the exam. One of my student's asthma would flare up as she approached exams. She knew to see her doctor beforehand to get the necessary opinion (that she was alright) and any needed medication. This way she would ease her mind and remove a potential distraction. Another student would develop a "tightening" in his chest. He knew this time that he need not go to the emergency room (again) because he was having an anxiety attack, not a heart attack. When symptoms occurred, he knew it was time to take a break, relax, visualize (the positive results) and then return to the routine. If, however, you experience new or prolonged physical symptoms, go see your doctor. It may be a symptom of something other than anxiety, which would be better addressed earlier rather than later.

Reflect upon those times when you were anxious. Know the signs and prepare to meet them. When you get anxious, take a break. Go to the movies. Jog around the reservoir. Do deep breathing. When I get anxious, I break into a rash. I don't eat or sleep much. On the day of an exam, I tend to perspire heavily. I know that I'm about to freak out when I feel that one cold bead of perspiration roll down from my underarm along my side. My ankles get weak and I can't seem to catch my breath. At this point, I have a choice: I can let the panic mount, consume me and become hysterical (losing precious time and points). Or, I can get to my seat quickly, close my eyes, catch my breath and begin chanting or praying while I breathe deeply. I choose the latter. By the time the exam booklets are passed around, I will have forced myself into composure, fixed my sights and unleashed my creative juices. The discipline we have been developing allows us to make the right choice.

Know the Law. There is a one-to-one relationship between *exam anxiety* and the extent of your legal knowledge. The less law you know, the more anxious you will become. The greater your preparation and resulting legal knowledge, the lower your anxiety. Given the 45-50 minutes you might have per essay or the 1.8 minutes per MBE question, you will have precious little time to waste trying to figure out the law. Writing concise, complete answers is a function of an ability quickly to *IDENTIFY THE ISSUES* and to *APPLY THE RELEVANT LAW.* Knowing the law cold will help you stay within the time constraints, and knowing the *right* law cold will help you increase your scores.

Know the "Right" Law. The bar exam tests more than the "black letter" law, those legal principles you learned in your first year of law school. If that were all that were tested, then just about everyone would pass. The bar exam also tests more than just the exception to the "black letter" law, although you must be able to identify applicable exceptions. More often than not, ***the bar exam tests an exception, to the exception, to the "black letter" law, which is usually that shade or nuance of the law that further defines rights and obligations.*** Consider, for example, a fact pattern which involves oral and written contract provisions and modifications in a commercial context. An aspect of the law that you would need to know is whether the Statute of Frauds (SOF) applies. Another level of knowledge required is whether there are applicable exceptions. The third level is knowing whether there are exceptions to this exception. You may get a point after noting the SOF's applicability. You will increase points by discussing exceptions or defenses to the SOF. You will gain even more points by identifying the applicability of the Uniform Commercial Code (UCC) and its provisions on contracts and contract modifications. The more levels of knowledge you display, the more points you can earn.

Now, if you became just a little anxious at the terminology and analytic issues presented above, you can begin to appreciate the interplay between exam anxiety and how much law you know. Eliminate anxiety connected to ignorance—*learn the law cold!*

How to Take the Bar Exam

There are techniques to answering bar exam questions. After having read more than my share of essay, MBE and multiple-choice questions and answers, I have gleaned certain patterns, tendencies and characteristics of successful exam-taking techniques. One such technique is the ability to *unlearn law school exam habits.*

Let's look at the last few years of your life. While in law school, you experienced a unique teaching modality—the Socratic method. You utilized a unique learning aid—the case book method. You more or less conquered a unique testing method—the hypothetical fact pattern. Before you can practice law, however, you are now told that you must pass an exam which is significantly different from those to which you have grown accustomed. Much of the bar exam is now standardized. You now need to know the correct or best answer for almost half of it. You need to forget the Socratic method and instead, listen for hours as a lecturer spoon feeds you the law. And, you must give up the case book approach for ready-made, detailed outlines of law and facts which, in some instances, can be reduced to a mnemonic formula for easy recall. If you can successfully make this transition, you are almost home. Below are listed a number of ways to get there.

Reading, Writing and Outlining. Upon receiving the exam itself and reading an essay question, your pen should be down. While reading it once, to get a panoramic view of the area (i.e., it is a contracts question, not criminal law), your pen is still down. If you see other students ferociously writing while your pen is down, you are not concentrating and you are losing time. As you read the bottom-line question, e.g., "What are the rights of the parties?," your pen should still be down.

During your *second reading* of the question, underline key words which raise an issue relative to the question. Note any applicable legal term or provision in the margin. Read *the bottom-line question* again and, this time, start your outline of the answer.

You may think that you should not take time to outline. *Think again.* It is the most efficient use of your time. The examiner is testing your analytical ability not verbosity and your answer must reveal how you resolve *all* issues. Because you know the law cold, and you have completed so many practice essays that you know the format well, you do not waste time groping for the right way to present your answer. You know the answers and your outline will aid your presentation of it.

There may come a time when you draw a blank or are asked to address an area of law that you did not study thoroughly. The worst thing you can do on exam day is to beat yourself up for not having done the work you should have done to answer a question, for which you now discover you are unprepared. You don't have time for that. Instead, this is the time for all the discipline you can muster. Go on to the questions you can answer. Save enough time to return to the one you skipped and reread it. Now concentrate harder. Something is bound to "click" and you will be able to respond. Maintain your discipline by outlining. <u>HINT:</u> If you are close to running out of time, and cannot complete a response, *include your outline as part of the answer to maximize your chance to receive some credit.*

Fear of Writing. Many people hesitate when expected to write their analysis because they believe they do not write well. Nobody is going after a Pulitzer Prize for the "Best Bar Exam Essay Answer." Write in complete sentences which make sense, contain the key legal words and phrases, and which show that you know what you are talking about. Consider Lenny H.

Lenny H.

Lenny wrote well, yet he was very self-conscious about his writing. He did not like to read his own writing, let alone to have others read it. Because of this self-consciousness, he felt that his writing had to be perfect.

To maintain "perfection," Lenny would take an inordinate amount of time composing his thoughts and phrases. To avoid this ordeal, he tended to avoid writing whenever possible, including writing out practice essay answers. Instead, he would just read the question and, at best, jot down a "quick and dirty" outline of his answer.

I remind students like Lenny of studies that show that many people do not write often, or well, and do not always put their thoughts together in a series of sentences that form logical paragraphs. I remind students that while law school requires that they know how to write, *few prizes are given for the best writing*. That grim fact is rightly reviewed as an educational disaster most of the time. But it is also an essential reminder that bar exams are not a showcase for literary perfectionism. To answer bar exam questions, students must know the law, spot the issues and formulate responsive answers. To avoid getting stuck, remember this advice; "Whenever you can shorten a sentence, do. And one always can. The best sentence? The shortest." Give your fear of writing a vacation. Don't let it keep you from passing the bar exam.

Fear of reading your writing. Suppose you wrote "X is *not* a holder in due course" instead of "X *is* a holder in due course." Catch such errors while you can correct them. Reread your essay answers and make sure that you schedule your time accordingly (between 5 and 7 minutes correction time per essay). If you haven't learned to edit yourself until now, this may be your last chance. Reread your answer to insure that your writing is legible and coherent. Look for misstatements, errors or omissions. This will be your last chance to do so.

Yes, we have no "red herrings." The facts provided in a bar exam question are either relevant to your ultimate answers or raise an issue to be addressed. Contrast this with law school exams, where some professors present "interesting" facts which, in the final analysis, hold little relevance to the issues presented. If you have not used most of the facts provided in a bar exam question, reread your answer. You might have missed an issue.

Conversely, rarely are there missing facts, but, if there are, it is for a reason. Often students write, "the question did not say whether the gun was licensed." Of course not! By omitting one or another fact, the bar exam tests your ability to make an assumption and proceed to a conclusion. The safe assumption to make is always the one that leads on to a difficult result, a new analytic problem that requires discussion. If you need a fact to complete your analysis, assume it, but assume that fact which will raise an issue. For example, if you assume a licensed gun, no issue is raised. Assume an unlicensed gun and you have an illegal possession charge to discuss.

Once is enough. Most bar exam essays have more than one part. You could be asked, "Were the numbered rulings correct?," "What rights, if any, does B have against S?," or "What are the rights and interests of H, S, D and F?". If you state the same answer on more than one part, e.g., H's rights are the same as D's, one of your answers is incomplete. No two parties will have identical rights. You need to reach into your memory banks to discern a legal nuance which will shade one of the parties' rights. If that fails, reread the fact pattern; another issue is lurking.

Assume nothing; take no prisoners. Assume that the person who grades your exam knows nothing. The bar exam is your time to display your legal acumen and knowledge. Define all legal terms, provisions and operations of law. Leave no gaps. There is no "trier of fact" who will resolve the issues you leave open. Students have a tendency to analyze an issue up to the point where they must draw a conclusion and then avoid stating that conclusion. Instead, they say it's up to the jury or judge. This is especially prevalent in criminal law or torts questions. You must state what a "trier of fact" or the charging party (e.g., prosecutor or plaintiff) would likely do based on the facts presented and the law which you then supply.

The "kitchen sink" . . . , in context. You must provide the definitions of legal terms, provisions and operations of law, *in the context of the issues presented.* If you feel compelled to tell the grader about the development of the law (because that's all you remember), resist it. Start with an issue. For example, in the context of a question dealing with merchants and an offer and an acceptance, neither of which contains the price term, you might begin your answer with a discussion of whether that missing term is fatal to the formation of the contract as between *these* parties. You now make a choice based on your legal knowledge: *either it is or it is not.* By simply framing the issue and stating a possible answer you may have garnered points; whereas a full-blown discussion of general principles of offers and acceptances and the common law "mirror image" rule, for example, would have probably resulted in none.

Key word in context. Bar exam graders look for *key words in context.* Where you know the legal term (e.g., gift *causa mortis*), use it. It makes it easier for the grader and provides greater insurance that you will receive credit.

Do make it easy for the graders. Don't make them struggle to read your essay. Grading is a part-time job for people with other full time jobs. Watch your handwriting. Dot your "i's" and "j's", don't use little circles. Do not cross out too much. *Be neat!*

Socrates is mortal . . . . Suppose you are asked, "What are A's causes of action"? If you simply list them and give nothing more, you are being conclusory. You have not given the grader *the information* which allows him/her to test your conclusion. In essence, you have not analyzed the issues. To maximize credit, you must identify the facts which give rise to the issue, which you will then analyze and use as a basis for your conclusion. Consequently, you cannot just say "Socrates is mortal." You must also state, "All men are mortal. Socrates is a man. *Therefore, Socrates is mortal.*" In applying this to a bar-like question, torts, for example, you don't want to leave your answer with the single statement that A has a cause of action for products liability, negligence and breach of implied warranty. You also want to demonstrate that proposition by stating, "why." For example, for products liability, the product had a defect and the defect caused the injury. The manufacturer's conduct fell below the standard of care (for negligence) and the product failed to perform as promised even though it was properly used (for breach of implied warranty).

The flip side. Whenever you discuss obligations, interests, charges or rights, discuss defenses and counter-defenses. For example, A can be charged with conspiracy. His defense might be that he renounced. Prosecutors would counter his defense by noting that his renunciation is ineffective because he failed to notify authorities. There are at least two sides to every case. Present them in your answer.

When in Rome . . . . When answering the essays, give the law of the jurisdiction administering the exam. Do not tell a New York grader what the law is in New Jersey. (A peril of studying simultaneously for two exams.) If you have an urge to compare and contrast what is done in other jurisdictions, *resist* it. You left that technique behind in law school.

The Mechanicals

Get there on time: In most jurisdictions, you have pre-assigned seats. But if possible, request a seat by the window if you need extra light, or have asthma; by the door if you have cystitis; by the radiator (in Feb.) if you get chills.

Every other page: Start writing your answer on page 3 of the exam booklet and write on every other page. That way, if you need to add information, you can do so on the opposite page and draw an arrow to where it is to be included. This keeps your answers looking neat and thoughtful.

Skip lines: Leave room to add words to sentences for the same reason as stated above.

Headers: Use topic headings to let the grader know that you have now concluded one topic and are ready to go to the next one.

Timepieces: Carry a good watch that works.

Fix-its: If you are prone to making major revisions, bring white-out, a small stapler, and scotch tape (if permitted). Otherwise, bring an ink eraser.

Be prepared: Carry a sweater in case it is cold. Carry pens that write, pencils which are sharpened and a pencil sharpener. Use the bathroom before the exam and again during breaks.

The Multiples: How Do You Get To Carnegie Hall?

If there is any magic to success on the MBEs or multiple-choice questions, it is appreciating that "repetition is the foundation of clarity." You must know the law cold and pay strict attention to detail. But you must also practice, practice, practice.

The repetition in answering hundreds, if not thousands of practice, MBE/multiple-choice questions is beneficial on a number of levels. After a while, you will begin to discern a pattern in the four choices. Two can be eliminated quickly. Of the remaining two, your ability to discern the "best" answer will be dependent upon how well you read the question. Remember: the exam tests legal nuances and shades. You can eliminate two choices easily because they tend to state black letter law which does not hold relevance to your fact pattern. The other two will both present applicable black letter law, but one will present a nuance that fits the facts better than the other. Thus, you will typically have to reread the question to determine which of the two remaining answers is the "best" one in the case of the MBEs or the "correct" one if it is a multiple-choice question. If you were to reread each of the MBE questions, for example, you will surely exceed the suggested time to be allotted to each of the 200 questions. Your goal in practice, therefore, is to get down to reading the questions only once, so that you can quickly eliminate the two wrong choices and zero in the best/correct one.

The repetition further assists you in attaining this goal by familiarizing you with the typical sentence structure, syntax and vocabulary of MBE/multiple-choice questions. This is especially relevant to students for whom English is a second language or who generally do not do well on reading comprehension exams or standardized tests, which the MBE certainly is both. Finally, questions from old exams are bound to reappear (if for no other reason than to determine relative difficulty. See above at p. 8). The more questions you answer in practice, the greater the likelihood of encountering a repeat on your exam.

*   *   *

One last piece of advice: I remember my bar exam day as if it were yesterday. I remember the *panic* felt, especially when I was about to enter the building. At that point, someone asked me "how many days do you have to file a complaint on a foreign corporation." When an answer did not jump from my lips, I almost fainted. The moral? Don't talk to strangers. Avoid the crowds at the test site. Go right to the room and breathe. Remember your *holiday* to come after the last day and your dream of becoming an attorney. ***Let your "Yes I can" attitude shine and your discipline prevail.***

CHAPTER SEVEN

THE BAR REVIEW COURSE

Law schools do not prepare students to take bar exams. At best, students are offered law courses, such as Domestic Relations and Trusts & Estates, which rely on the type of local law that bar exams do test. This is especially true of the *local* law schools, as opposed to the *national* ones, which utilize majority view, model law or federal rules when discussing legal principles. As a consequence, the commercial bar review industry was developed to meet students' unmet need of having to learn local law and learn it fast to be successful on the bar exam.

Distilled to their essence, the review courses provide students with the most up-to-date version of the law tested on a given bar exam. They provide sample questions, either from old exams or questions constructed in the style of a bar exam; and they give guidance on test-taking techniques, study habits and scheduling. This is true for general review courses, as well as those which specialize in particular parts of the exam, for example, MBE preparation courses.

Going It Alone

Some people do choose to go it alone and forego the traditional bar review course. They are rarely first-time takers, who typically need the structure, guidance and materials provided by the review courses. They are most often candidates who have previously taken a bar exam and who have previously experienced the challenges of preparation. If you decide against taking a bar review course, make sure you have the following:

- *practice questions and/or old exams;*
- *updated legal information;*
- *sufficient intestinal fortitude to stay the course.*

You can get sample questions and model answers from previous exams from your state boards of bar examiners. Consult *Appendix B* for details. As noted earlier, candidates can get sample MBE questions from the National Conference of Bar Examiners. Your local law library can provide access to the most recent pronouncements on the areas of law that will be tested on the bar exam. In certain instances, the search may be facilitated by legal publishing houses which can now provide the law of certain jurisdictions on CD-ROM. For example, Butterworth Legal Publishers will provide CDs on thirty-four (34) jurisdictions, including Virgin Islands law. Their number is (800) 542-0957. Lawyers Cooperative Publishing will provide CDs on New York and federal law. They can be reached at (800) 762-5272. West Publishing similarly provides CDs for New York. Call them at (800) 255-2549, ext. 175.

In addition, there are review courses for in-home use which offer study programs for the bar exam to be used on your personal computer. They provide outlines, lectures, teaching questions, and bar simulations. The costs vary and program availability tends to be limited to a few states. Law school newspapers often run advertisements for these courses. Check Reed Law Group, discussed below. They provide in-home study programs, along with the more traditional course. For the CD-ROM or in-home programs, you will obviously need access to a personal computer, one with CD-ROM capabilities.

A Review of the Reviews

If you do choose to take a bar review course, do your homework first. I am often asked to recommend a bar review course. My response is always the same. ***Take the course which best fits your personality and study style.*** You hear about the courses while in law school. You see their tables in the school lobby or student lounge. Many courses have student representatives who may seek you out. If you are out of law school, you can check your local legal periodical or write to the bar examiners. Although they will not endorse particular courses, the Board may distribute lists of them.

Check the courses out before signing up. There are review courses for the "intellectual" which give you more "black letter law" than you need to practice law, let alone, to pass the bar exam. Other courses will have reviewed prior exams and the areas which have been tested to predict which subjects and legal principles will appear on up-coming exams. There are bar review courses which specialize in various types of exam techniques, e.g., mnemonic devices. And some bar courses try to combine elements of all the above and then some.

Notwithstanding the variations, most of these courses have the same basic structure.

There are two parts to most bar review courses, live or taped lectures on the substantive law and practice questions to be answered under simulated exam conditions and mailed in for grading. The lectures are the core of most courses. Unlike law school, there is little class participation. The majority of the time will consist of note-taking while listening to 3-4 hour lectures. Each lecture will usually begin with a hypothetical question. The remainder of the lecture could involve the analysis and resolution of the question using applicable legal principles. Although there may be preparatory chapters which can be read prior to a lecture, the lecture notes are the primary teaching tools and repetition is the key to learning.

First, you read the designated courses materials before class. Then the same information is presented to you by a law school professor or practitioner during the lecture. You take relevant notes on it. You hear a discussion of it. When you go home, you review the information, rewrite it and outline it.

The mail-in essay questions continue the repetition, by testing the student's understanding of the relevant legal principles. Answering the mail-in questions may seem a painful experience, but it is extremely worthwhile. Your scores will be low at first (partly because course administrators don't want you to get too confident too early); and sometimes the comments (which graders are encouraged to write plenty of) may not seem too fair or accurate. The exercise is nevertheless quite beneficial, in that your grade lets you see how you stand in relation to your peers. Practice exams are graded on the same scale as the bar exam. If the essay is graded from 1-10, your practice exam will be returned with an overall score using the same scale. You will also see how that score was arrived at. You will see what part of your answer was worth a point, what part was worth half a point and so on. The exercise also provides you the opportunity to determine the areas you have mastered and the extent to which you need to deal with exam anxiety.

Some courses offer students the opportunity to take a simulated bar exam. Take it if offered. Up until that point, students may have had only their past performance on law school exams to predicate their future performance on the bar exam. Your response to the bar exam may be quite different. One student recalls that during the MBE, "the questions began to float off the page." She had not previously sat through a full day of MBEs and was not prepared for the fatigue, boredom and anxiety she would later experience. A "dry run" will inform you of ways in which the pressures may affect you. *Knowing what to expect allows you to plan ahead.*

Take cost, for instance. These courses are not cheap. Shop around before you buy. The costs can start around $1,000 for the basics and with "extras," those costs can increase by up to another $1500. The extras can be obtained as an adjunct to a larger course or through an independent program. Many programs offer repeater courses, multistate workshops, essay writing workshops, special lectures for out-of-state students and for those taking two exams, and a class on the Multistate Professional Responsibility Examination (MPRE). Take advantage of "trial" offers before you put your money down and if money is an object, find out about scholarships, discounts for those going into public service, and employment as a bar review sales representative. This way you can get the course for free or at a discount and receive a bounty for each student you sign up. For example, West Bar Review, the "new kid on the block" (see below p. 51) is hiring student representatives. To apply, contact West at (212) 535-6811. A prospective employer may pay for the course. One student in need of funds was able to get his local bar association to guarantee payment which he would make when he started his post-exam employment. Be creative. All they can say is *no*, and they just might say *yes*.

Popular Choices

Below is a partial listing of the courses offered nationally and a sampling of these in New York and California (the two most popular bar exams). To find local courses, you should contact your local bar association, the legal periodicals in your city (especially in November and May, when bar results are typically published); or check your school's newspaper or the National Jurist Magazine. Ads for these courses are bound to appear in student-oriented periodicals.

New courses come and go. Old ones fade. Make sure you take a recognized course. While fraud has yet to be major concern in the industry, it occurs. Some courses are quick to boast a high pass rate for all of its students, regardless of which exam they took. Make sure that the pass rate reflects those students in that course who passed the same bar exam for which you are preparing. For example, if you are taking the Tennessee bar exam, make sure that a course boasting of a 90% pass rate is talking about its students who sat for the Tennessee bar. Check it out thoroughly. Some programs have been caught inflating or misrepresenting their numbers. If you are at all concerned about a course, check with the bar association and the grievance committees (attorneys usually run these courses) and the Better Business Bureau.

Below are some of the national courses and local ones for New York and California. There is no particular significance to the order. It is more or less alphabetical. Moreover, inclusion of a course in this list is by no means an endorsement.

*   *   *

National Courses

BAR/BRI
1500 Broadway
New York, New York 10036
1-800-472-8899

BAR/BRI offers "full service" courses in 45 states. Its courses cover local law and multistate subjects. A three-day intensive program on the MBE which includes a simulated MBE and a day of "subject by subject" analysis of questions is also offered.

BAR/BRI's literature describes its program as consisting of:

> *Comprehensive, concise outlines prepared by BAR/BRI's staff of lecturers. These totally bar exam oriented summaries cover all subjects tested on both the local and Multistate portions of the exam. Simulated testing sessions for both local and Multistate portions of the exam will be given. Selected Multistate questions are computer graded and selected essays are individually graded and critiqued by local attorneys.*

PMBR
1-800-523-0777

PMBR calls itself the "Multistate Specialist." It offers a three-day program in 42 states, including D.C. The program's literature states: *"Day 1 is the 'Trial Run,' on which day a preliminary MBE is administered. Days 2 and 3 consist of an intensive MBE review, which involves the analysis of the practice exam questions from Day 1."*

REED LAW GROUP, LTD.
28 Rivers Bend Court
Barrington, Illinois 60010
1-800-852-3926

Reed Law Group offers both full bar review courses for Illinois and Texas and live or in-home courses on the Multistate. According to its materials, Reed provides: *"Realistic Multistate exams created from recent issues tested regularly on the latest MBE's. Your answers will be computer-graded, comparing your scores to actual scores achieved by those who took the MBE in the past."*

THE SKILLMAN METHOD
484 Lake Park Avenue
Suite 364
Oakland, California 94610
(212) 628-5109 (in New York City); (510) 452-1415

The Skillman Method offers a general bar exam preparation course in Manhattan, the San Francisco Bay Area, Los Angeles, and Boston. Their program consists of a basic seven hour course, "How to Prepare for the Bar Exam"; and covers all phases of exam preparation, including scheduling, outlining bar materials, the MBE exam, and exam writing and legal analysis. A six-week "Intensive Bar Course" is also offered. Students take an in-class examination weekly and meet with the faculty regularly for individual instruction. Every paper turned in is critiqued in writing, line-by-line. Students also receive an audiotape on exam writing.

Private instruction videos and audiotapes are available.

SMH BAR REVIEW
1-800-BAR-EXAM

SMH is offered in 23 jurisdictions. In addition to providing lectures, books and practice exams, SMH offers a "computer diagnostic analysis." It describes this feature as follows:

> *The full SMH Computer Diagnostic Analyses (CDA) compiles your performance on practice questions given throughout the course .... Every SMH student receives a floppy disk containing SMH's proprietary software containing the full Computer Diagnostic Analyses. With this tool, you can input your answers to 1,600 of SMH's practice questions at home and receive the full CDA report.*

WEST BAR REVIEW
A Subsidiary of the West Publishing Company
c/o 330 East 75th Street, 33rd Floor
New York, New York 10021
(212) 535-6811

The West Bar Review calls itself "the nation's newest and most experienced bar review." West is headed by Stan Chess, the long-time president of BAR/BRI, and Steve Levine, BAR/BRI's former national director. Besides Chess and Levine, other West Bar Review lecturers include Harvard Professor Arthur Miller and John Moye, who teaches by using rock n'roll tunes.

Popular Choices - New York

PIEPER NEW YORK - MULTISTATE BAR REVIEW, LTD.
1517 Franklin Avenue
Mineola, New York 11501
(516) 747-4311

Using "the Pieper Active-Teaching" style, John Pieper personally prepares students through lectures and essays. Pieper is best known for his mnemonic devices, or memory aids, which promotional materials describe as part of the "Pieper Difference." His materials note that the Pieper course is the only bar review geared exclusively to the New York bar exam: *Taking the bar exam is, in many ways, an endurance test. So, to be successful, the seven week bar review period must be thought of as training for a marathon . . . . John Pieper is that coach, and Pieper Bar Review is the course that makes you meet the challenge.*

Tutorials

SUPPLEMENTAL BAR REVIEW   TUTORIAL PROGRAM
PALS   Alaska Bar Association
42 West 44th Street   P.O. Box 100279
New York, New York 10036   Anchorage, Alaska 99510-0279
(212) 382-6600   (907) 272-7469

I make special mention of these programs because of their dedication to assisting *disadvantaged* students through the bar exam process. I helped to design and run the New York program which has consistently reached pass rates of well above the average. In some years, it has come within percentage points of the overall state pass rate. The New York program, modeled after one started in Chicago, focuses on improving essay-writing and test-taking skills rather than concentrating on substantive legal concepts. Students meet as a group one afternoon each week for six weeks prior to the bar exam to hear lectures on such topics as organization. They then take sample exam questions for later review. Each student is assigned a mentor who provides exam feedback and support. These programs stand as models which other bar associations and schools have adopted or are considering. Check your local bar association to see if they have or are willing to adopt one.

*   *   *

Make the most out of the review course you choose. If you have questions, ask. If you need guidance, request it. Do it after class or call them later on. Get your money's worth. ***Remember: Your success is their success.***

lectures on such topics as organization. They then take sample exam questions for later review. Each student is assigned a mentor who provides exam feedback and support. These programs stand as models which other bar associations and schools have adopted or are considering. Check your local bar association to see if they have or are willing to adopt one.

*　　　*　　　*

Make the most out of the review course you choose. If you have questions, ask. If you need guidance, request it. Do it after class or call them later on. Get your money's worth. ***Remember***: ***Your success is their success.***

CHAPTER EIGHT

NOT FOR THE MINORITY STUDENT ONLY

The challenge of staying in a *"Yes I Can"* mode is especially daunting for minority candidates. Throughout law school, they hear about low minority pass rates and witness bar exam failures of their classmates. Coupled with the general disaffirming portrayals of minorities found in law school and elsewhere, many students of color begin to believe, as early as first year of law school, that they will not pass the bar. In too many instances, this self-defeatism becomes self-fulfilling. They believe that they *cannot* pass so they *do not* pass. Thus, if any persons are in need of the *"Yes I Can"* attitude presented in Chapter One, it may be these students.

We take the time here to explore the added concerns and challenges which some of these students may experience as they work to develop the more pro-ductive attitude they will need to prepare for and pass the bar exam. Because self-defeatism, however, is an equal opportunity attitude—not exclusive to stu-dents of color—I urge *all* people to continue reading this chapter. It holds rel-evance for women, the physically challenged, economically disadvantaged, the first generation professional, the orthodox, the older, or the gay or lesbian can-didate for the bar. In effect, any person who has been challenged by real or perceived roadblocks in their lives, often brought on by forces beyond their control (like being from a dysfunctional family), may find solace and direction in the succeeding pages.

Today's "Special"

Rasheeda J.[2]

Rasheeda, an African-American woman, was a first
generation high school, college and law school graduate
and the "star" of her immediate and extended family of

---

[2] Any reference to race, ethnicity, gender or culture is an intentional effort to raise important issues.

grandparents, aunts, cousins, and siblings. She was iden-
tified early in life as someone who was "special." Her
family could not be prouder of her accomplishments and
because of her "specialness," Rasheeda was looked up
to and sometimes envied by family members.

In school she was identified as "gifted" and placed
in special programs. In elementary school, she was placed
in "IGC" classes for the "intellectually gifted child." In
intermediate school, she was placed in the "S.P." (spe-
cial progress) classes and allowed to skip a grade, and in
high school, she was in the "honors" program. Because
of these placements, Rasheeda was elevated in status by
school administrators and teachers and often envied by
other students. As a result of her enriched education,
Rasheeda was articulate, well read and quite "cultured."

Although Rasheeda was an "A" student, her SAT
scores were lower than she needed to gain direct admis-
sion into the Ivy League College of her choice. She did
get admitted, however, under the college's "special" ad-
missions program. Her college grades were good, but
again, her scores on the LSAT were too low to get her
into the Ivy League Law School of her choice. She did
get into a good law school, though not Ivy, through its
"special" admissions program.

Although debate still rages over *special admissions* programs (programs
which seek to increase numbers of minority and/or disadvantaged law students),
there can be little argument that the *specialness* of these later programs is not
the *specialness* of Rasheeda's early education. There was a time in education
when *special* was understood (rightly or wrongly) to mean *better than*; when
special programs or *s.p. (special progress)* classes involved curricula designed
to enrich and enhance the innate abilities of the student. The *specialness* then
was a validation of the person as a whole. The programs were designed to
bring out what the student had within.

Special has now come to mean (rightly or wrongly) *less good*, e.g., *spe-*

cial education. This *specialness* means that the student is needy or lacking and that the missing piece(s) is to be found outside of the individual. As such, today's *special* programs are often viewed as stigmas, as evidence that the students could not make it on their own.

During Rasheeda's educational career, she went from being *special* and seen as *better than*, to being *special* and considered *less good*. And this later *specialness* was most pronounced in law school because, for the first time in her life, Rasheeda was not a *star*.[3]

Rasheeda called me to follow-up on a statement that I had made at a lecture. She wanted to know what I meant when I said, "Assume the bar exam is biased." Without knowing it, Rasheeda wanted me to confirm her suspicions and thereby validate her actions.

I had often seen the mix of emotions experienced by Rasheeda. Students are afraid that they will fail and find it more comforting to ascribe that failure to something beyond their control, in this case *bias*. And they encourage themselves, when and if they do fail, to believe that it was because of what was beyond their control—*bias*. As a result, many students will not develop the positive attitude needed to believe themselves capable of passing; nor will they design an effective study schedule and develop the discipline to stick to it. They conclude, "Why bother? The exam is biased." They do not study, they fail the exam and the self-fulfilling prophecy comes to pass.

There are things in life that we can control and those we cannot. At this point in her life, Rasheeda could no more control any of the institutional biases she may have been facing than she could control the stereotypical thinking of others as to her *specialness*. She could control, however, the way in which she responded to them. Unfortunately, her response had set the stage for failure.

Rasheeda J. (continued)

Rasheeda's first year at law school was traumatic.
Not only was she greeted with what seemed to be only
one-dimensional portrayals of people of color in her
casebook and lecture topics, she found herself in the

---

[3]Nothing herein should be viewed as a condemnation of "special" programs, for the author is a proud product of a number of them.

middle of the debate on the fairness and efficacy of "special admissions" programs. She tried to stay out of this fray, as she worked hard, determined to make law review.

Despite her efforts, her first semester grades were the lowest grades she had ever received in her life. In an effort to find out what happened, Rasheeda talked with her friends, many of whom were minority group members who drew together to give each other comfort, only to find out that their grades were as low, if not lower than hers.

She spoke to professors and advisors; but still she couldn't figure out what she was doing wrong. She worked hard and put in long hours; briefed every case and answered the questions in the notes which followed and in the hand-outs. Yet, things did not improve. No matter how well she thought she wrote, Rasheeda's legal memoranda needed major revisions. Regardless of how well spoken she was most of the time, when Rasheeda was called upon in class, she could not seem to get the right words out. And no matter how hard she studied, her grades remained the same—low.

Since nothing she tried seemed to improve matters, Rasheeda began to wonder whether there was "something" at work that was beyond her control. Upperclass students told her it was racism and no matter how hard she studied she would get the same grades. It had happened to them.

Slowly, but surely, she began spending more time on other matters, such as the minority students association, even though the frictions existing in that group were tiresome. She took a job in the second year and her life took on a new and much more demanding dimension, when her boyfriend wanted more "quality time."

As she approached third year, she began to pay closer

attention to the stories of how and why people of color
were failing the bar and less attention to those third year
courses which are tested on the exam. Her doubts about
her ability to pass grew as she heard of the failure of
other people of color who everyone thought would pass.
She ever so slowly started turning her would-be produc-
tive energies into "No, I Can't" laments.

Is the Bar Exam Biased?

Treat this question like one found on the Multistate. The possible choices
for the *best* answer are:

A) Not at all

B) Probably not

C) More than likely

D) Totally

True to the general MBE pattern, two choices can be easily eliminated.
You can easily eliminate A) because it would be reasonable to conclude that, to
a certain extent, everything is a product of culture, and that cultural biases are
bound to be expressed consciously or unconsciously, overtly or covertly in
whatever the endeavor. This proposition, as it relates to the bar exam, is supported by the seminal study conducted by the National Commission on Testing
and Public Policy. In its report, "From Gatekeeper to Gateway: Transforming
Testing in America" (1990), the Commission found that:

No test can be wholly free from cultural bias, for as prod-
ucts of culture tests are permeated with cultural implica-
tions in both form and content. We must stop pretending
that any single standard test can illuminate equally well
the talents and help promote the learning of people from
dramatically different backgrounds.

You can also quickly eliminate D), that the exam is totally biased, because
the bar is not like the old *poll test* which many states imposed to keep Blacks
from voting. These tests, like determining the number of jelly beans in a jar,
were not passable because they were arbitrarily imposed and capriciously graded.

Conversely, Blacks and other *disadvantaged* people have been passing the bar exam since its inception and continue to do so in numbers that would belie the existence of a totally biased exam.

Now you are left with B) and C) from which to choose the *best* answer. To do so, I refer you to Chapter Six where we discussed ways in which to answer a question when a critical fact or piece of information is missing. In that case, we said to supply your own fact or information; that which would lead to a difficult result and a new analytical problem that requires further discussion or action. In effect, choose the "worst case scenario." In so doing, you give yourself more to talk about, more options from which to choose and you lessen the possibility that you have chosen incorrectly. In the context of whether the bar exam is biased, if you chose B), that the exam is probably not biased, then further discussion is foreclosed, along with the option of taking prophylactic or corrective action, just in case you are wrong.[4] If you chose C), that the exam is more than likely biased, then you reach a result that will allow you to take the action you need to overcome: You work harder; at the appropriate time, you may choose to engage in collective activity;[5] and you turn the *disadvantage* into an ***advantage.***

---

[4] Here, the missing fact or information is the evidence or proof of bias or the lack thereof. Surprisingly, there have been relatively few studies of minority performance on the bar exam. Of the existing studies, there is agreement that there is a disparity between minority and White performance. There is substantial disagreement as to the reason. Studies of the California exam identify LSAT scores and GPAs as the predictors of success on the exam, not race, gender or ethnicity. Experts studying the Florida exam disagree. In support of their argument, they cite those studies which find that the LSAT scores themselves are biased measures. In addition, they found that the linguistic and culturally-specific fact patterns of the exam account for some of the disparity.

[5] In 1974, a group of black lawyers petitioned the New York Court of Appeals to appoint a commission to study the bar exam. They argued that the exam violated the 14th Amendment because it had a discriminatory impact on black candidates and could not be shown to be "job-related." The Court did some tinkering but denied the request. In 1988, the Chief Judge appointed the New York State Judicial Commission on Minorities, chaired by the late Ambassador Franklin H. Williams, which reviewed the pass rates of law graduates of color on the bar exam. Because its preliminary analysis showed significant disparities among the racial groups, in 1990, the Commission called for a more comprehensive review of the exam for bias. That review is now being conducted by the Law School Admissions Council which has undertaken a nationwide study of minority performance on the bar exam.

Advantage: Yours

> *Milagros L.*
>
> *Milagros was an ideal student to tutor. She was re-*
> *sponsive to my critique. She worked hard and completed*
> *her assignments on time. She came from a very proud*
> *Mexican-American family, who prayed for the first law-*
> *yer in the family to pass the bar exam. Milagros, how-*
> *ever, did not seem to be as proud of her family as they*
> *were of her, given the way she spoke of them.*
>
> *To our surprise, Milagros failed the exam. Upon re-*
> *view of her paper, she discovered, with amazement, that*
> *she had written some of her essay answers in Spanish.*

The obvious and easy lesson for Milagros was the importance of rereading her answers, and managing her stress. But the harder and not-so-obvious lesson was that she needed to look at the reasons why she was putting down her family, her culture and ethnicity. Milagros could run from who and what she was, but, as her exam answer showed, she could not hide from it. Her energies would have been better expended in embracing her ethnicity and turning her negative energy into a positive force; the type of force needed to pass an exam, raise a family or change a country. In effect, Milagros needed to turn her perceived disadvantage into an advantage.

There are many examples of this type of *conversion* throughout our history. For the longest time in our country, one of the worst things you could call an African-American was *black*. To be *black* was to be bad. But the political and cultural awareness and pride brought on by the political upheaval of the 1960s changed that. To be *Black* was to be good. That shifting produced monumental change in our society, spurred on a movement, and released a spirit in a people and a country which is still felt to this day.

For some of us, knowing our history will help us to understand our place in it and gain the necessary appreciation of it. To know that history is to acknowledge that we still live in an era of *firsts* in the law and in our society—the first African-American Governor since Reconstruction; the first Puerto Rican Congresswoman; the first elected Asian-American judge in New York State;

the first American Indian Senator; the first openly-lesbian Federal District Court Judge. We further need to appreciate that the *firsts* in the law come after mere decades of acceptance as full-fledged members of the Bar.

Ben G.

Ben's parents immigrated to the United States from China when he was six years old. He was one of my students in the Supplemental Bar Review Program described earlier. During the first few sessions, it became clear to me that Ben was feeling uncomfortable. He was the only Asian-American in a group of Blacks, Hispanics and two Whites. At our second individual session, I asked Ben about his apparent discomfort. Although he denied it, he did mention that he was not getting much out of the lectures and that his practice exams answers were consistently low.

Ben's low performance continued. With the exam approaching in less than a month's time, I confronted him: was he uncomfortable about being the only Asian-American in the course? He finally admitted that he did not like being there because everyone thought that Asian-Americans were "smart." And here he was in a program for people with "special" needs.

Many of us feel the need to single-handedly dispel stereotypes of us or our people or to live up to someone else's expectations, no matter how unrealistic. This is especially true for *first generation* college or law school graduates, no matter what their race, religion, gender or sexual orientation. To many of them, everything they do is a reflection on their race or group. They have the need to be the *model minority* (as in Ben's case) or a *credit* to the race.

It is not easy for some to let go of a group identity or those aspects of it that can cause them to become dysfunctional. There's a feeling of loss and betrayal. But you have to be who you are, not who others think you should be. To do otherwise is to work against yourself and you don't have time for that, especially during the bar preparation period. Ben realized that his discomfort stemmed from his feeling that he had failed in not living up to the *model minority* stereotype and that his participation in a group of students who were ostensibly in need of *special* attention was evidence of his failure. What he did not realize was that his discomfort inhibited his interaction with the other students (some of whom had much to offer him) and diverted his attention from the information being shared. What a waste!

The *"Yes, I Can"* attitude speaks directly to those who are first generation. Like so many of them, Ben focused more on the stigmatizing aspects of being first generation, than on those aspects of this status that were affirming and optimistic. To shift his focus, we looked at all he had accomplished despite the perceived disadvantages and we looked at all his family had accomplished despite their humble circumstances. We then looked at how similar the other students were to him in their accomplishments and in their goals. While Ben didn't have an epiphany, he did attain a greater appreciation of what it meant to be first generation. He realized that reaching one of the pinnacles in this society, becoming a lawyer, indicated a reservoir of determination, a collective *"Yes, I Can"* attitude, and commitment from which he could draw strength. Armed with this knowledge, Ben realized something else—his goal of passing the bar exam.

*   *   *

So, yes, I tell students to assume the exam is biased. I also tell them not to waste another moment on the question. Although you may have tapped new sources of energy with your *"Yes I Can"* outlook, neither your time nor your energy is boundless. And with the exam fast approaching there are only two available options. Take it, or don't take it.

You take it, of course, if for no other reason than you have paid your money for the bar review course, possibly relocated to the test state and have begun readying yourself for the challenge. And, you are not ready for your spouses, families and banks (to whom you owe thousands in student loans) to come after you with a vengeance if you cop out.

But there's another reason to take it. You take it because you have not made it this far without knowing how to overcome the challenges of bias. You made it through first year despite your low LSAT scores. You finished exams despite being blind and needing a reader. You made the moot court team despite having English as a second language. You graduated law school despite an absentee father or a substance-addicted mother. You take it because *you've come too far to let anyone or anything turn you around.*

CHAPTER NINE

THE PRE-EXAM CRUNCH

Too many students believe something magical happens on July 4th that will make them get serious about preparation for a bar exam scheduled for the end of July. Or, that on February 1st they will be transformed into *lean mean study machines*, in time for the end of February exam. Unfortunately, few of these students realize that if they wait until then, they may have waited too long. Consider Karen R.

> ### Karen R.
>
> *Graduation day for Karen was May 13th. It took her a few days to settle down afterwards. She had to move back home to Chicago. She had to say good-bye to new friendships and reestablish old ones. Karen was to begin her bar review course on the 22nd, but she missed the first week. She explained it away as part of her transition.*
>
> *It was now June 3rd. Karen still had her bar exam application to complete and although she was going to class regularly, she had fallen behind and had to take time out from on-going preparation to catch up.*
>
> *By June 15th, Karen still had not caught up and she had not completed the first mail-in exam question, although she did read it over and it seemed manageable. On top of the catching up, completing the daily lecture preparation and taking the overdue exam, Karen was having trouble understanding certain subjects, like Property and Trust and Estates. Moreover, friends and relatives kept bugging her to be more available. "You can't study 24 hours a day," they admonished her.*
>
> *To accommodate them she took the next two weekends off, telling herself, "July 4th is when I'll get it together."*

Let's take another look at the schedules presented in Chapter Four and the calendars in *Appendix C*. Now look at the one on the following page.

JULY

SUN	MON	TUES	WED	THURS	FRI	SAT
		4	*5*	*6*	*7*	*8*
9	*10*	*1,*	*12*	*13*	*14*	*15*
16	*17*	*1ε*	*19*	*20*	*21*	*22*
23	*24*	*2ɔ*	*26*	*27*	*28*	*29*
		Bar Exam Week				
30	*31*					

Get the picture? By July 4th, you will begin to notice that everything has begun to accelerate. The days will fly by because you are now more cognizant of time. The bar review courses will schedule extra days and hours so that *they* can catch-up. The intensive practice sessions will begin now because they are scheduled to conclude right before the exam. Reviewing and outlining will become imperatives. There will be little time for cramming. You will have all you can do to remain on top of things. If you wait until July 4th to get it together, you are left with only three weeks before the exam to do your catch-up, your practice exams and your review—*not a lot of time*. Therefore, I repeat: if you wait until July 4th or some other such "magical" date, you may have waited too long.

The bar exam is like any other of life's challenges, with its huge amount of stress, vulnerability to fantasy and potential for backsliding. As noted in previous chapters, passing the exam, like meeting those other challenges, is up to you. How, where, when and with whom you study are up to you, and the earlier you decide to have it all "come together" the better your chances for success. Nothing magical will enable you to catch up. It will take time and study.

Therefore, early in your schedule, you should plan a group therapy session with your study buddy about cold feet: experiences before your first day in a new school (at least as devastating as any bar exam); your first real date; your first any number of things. You'll then be able to see that you are not alone and that you must force yourself into the orderly schedule you had planned. The worst thing you can do is to withdraw into superstition, fantasy and magic and let things pile up. Unless you make it go away long before the magical date your mind tries to set for you, it will kill you. The answer to magic is work.

Don't wait for July 4th or its winter equivalent to "get it together." Instead, make that date one of holidays or vacation days you take off during your study period. Go to the parades, the slopes, the movies, the park. *But do not wait until then to get it all together.*

*   *   *

Having Said All That

Let's say that you now find yourself with only twenty or so days in which to *get it all together.* What do you do? Don't panic! Read Chapters One, Four, Five and Six of this book. You must now plan your life down to the nanosecond. Use one of the work calendars in *Appendix D* to schedule every day from July 5th (February 1st) through the bar exam. You even schedule study time for the days between each section of the exam. Identify the topics which appear on every bar exam and devote your remaining time to them, along with the multistate topics. Do practice questions daily—50 MBEs and one or two essays. Pay close attention to the sample answers. They are great sources of information.

If you make your mind up to "do it," and adopt *The Program* and stick to it, *you can still pass the bar exam*!

CHAPTER TEN

TWO BAR EXAMS

When I am asked whether a student should take two (or more) bar exams, I answer, *"NO."* My answer is contrary to popular wisdom. And despite my advice, you may follow that wisdom.

Fear Of Failing

Let us suppose that you are considering taking the New York and New Jersey bar exams in July. New Jersey is thought to be the easier of the two exams as it only tests a handful of subjects as compared to New York's twenty-something. You could therefore conceivably give New York your "quality" study time and only review New Jersey law. Moreover, the bar examiners in both states have made logistics easy by permitting students to take New York on Tuesday, the Multistate for both states on Wednesday and the New Jersey part (or Connecticut and Massachusetts, for that matter) on Thursday. *"So, why not take both?,"* you ask. The answer is simple.

Few people have a legitimate, business-related reason for admission to practice in two states at the same time, least of all recent law school graduates. In addition, most people have already identified the specific state in which they will practice by the time they are ready to take a bar exam. Given all this and the fact that the profession places no premium on multiple admissions, there is really no professional reason to take both. Yet, many people do. They do because, for some of them, the thought of failure is terrifying. And since failing the bar exam is such a public event, there would be no way of hiding the fact. Having a backup (the real reason people take more than one exam), gives a candidate another shot at passing. As the rationale goes, it is better to take two and pass one, than to take one and pass none. By taking two bar exams, students are trying to hedge their bets so that even if they fail their prime bar exam, they can still be considered a winner by passing the other.

For some people, such a *hedge* is dangerous. It plants a seed of doubt as to their ability to pass. As we discussed earlier, there is enough external disaffirmance around us already. If we are not careful, doubts can seep in, water and nourish that internal seed, shifting our positive thoughts of passing to negative images of failing. Although people will tell you how easy it is to prepare for two exams, you could be faced with a situation where the logistics of taking the two exams may require more time than anticipated; the application process may become more intrusive than realized; and the money to pay for both may become more problematic than desired. In no time, you may be diverted from study for your primary exam to attend to the details of the secondary exam, resulting in the very thing which you feared and for which you were hedging—*failing.*

Keep your energies focused on passing. You can learn the right answers. You have been lectured by the *gurus* of bar passage. And you have adopted and stuck to **The Program.** Why give yourself a reason to fail?

*   *   *

You Can Lead A Horse To Water

Despite the above admonition, you have to judge your ability to handle two exams. If you decide to take both, be wise in your choice. Some bar review courses offer workshops on taking two exams. Check them out. At a minimum, however, do not take an exam that will cause you to worry about out-of-state accommodations, added financial outlays and elaborate travel plans. Do not take an exam that will require you to study more than you are prepared to, and do not take exams which are considered of equal difficulty, e.g., New York *and* California.

CHAPTER ELEVEN

STOPPING THE CYCLE OF FAILURE

You may have taken the exam so often that you've given up hope of ever passing it. You may have tried different review courses, and workshops, even tried hypnosis, but you still haven't passed the bar after three attempts. Or, maybe you're still feeling the pain of having failed it on your first try. Whatever your situation, there is a discernible reason why you failed.

To end the cycle of failure or to stop one before it starts, you need to search your soul now to find out the reason(s) you allowed yourself to be diverted from your primary goal of passing the exam and from the work you knew you had to do to get there. If you do not choose to take the time now, you will eventually be forced to. The same ambivalence that was expressed through your failure this time will be there the next time you take the exam, and the seeds of a future failure will have been sown and watered.

The First Time

The bar exam has often been compared to a *rite of passage*, where a young person must pass a test or make a showing of his/her worthiness to become a full-fledged member of the social group or religious order. The comparison, however, is misleading. True rites often involve long-term preparation, a pairing of the initiate with an elder, who will determine when the youngster is *ready*, and the investment of the entire community in the success of the undertaking. If the bar exam and its process had the structural supports found in true rites of passage, we would probably see fewer people failing it. The problem is that it does not.

If the ten weeks or so spent in preparation for the bar exam were enhancing the knowledge and honing the skills learned the last three years in law school, you could consider yourself to have had the long-term preparation typical of most passage rites. They do not. While your analytical abilities are needed for the bar, you have to apply and articulate them in new and different ways.

Some people need more than ten weeks to learn how to do this. Because there is no elder, teacher, sensei, or coach to let you know when you are ready, the only way some people find out that they were not is when they receive their notice of failure.

If the law schools, bar associations, examiners and the like had a stake in your individual success on the bar, the exam would again come closer to that of a true rite of passage. Most do not. It would seem that the only members of the legal community invested in your passing the bar exam are the review courses. But while some do care, their interest is largely financial and it comes at the end of your training which for some candidates is too late. Rarely do law schools or bar association play an active part in preparing you for the bar exam. While there are exceptions, like CUNY and Turo law schools and various local bar associations, when you graduate, you are pretty much on your own in opening the *gates* to the profession. Little or no assistance is provided by the gatekeepers.

Given this, you should not worry if you were ill-prepared for your first try. The fact that you got through it is a plus. Consider it a dry run. Now you know what it is like, what is expected and how you reacted to the pressures. You can use that knowledge to go right into **The Program** for the next exam. You can also take solace from the finding of the New York State Judicial Commission on Minorities which surveyed litigators on their bar exam experiences. One finding, which relied on responses of law school graduates from all over the United States and included test-takers over many years, was that the average number of bar pass efforts for all those surveyed, regardless of race, was *two*.

For the Above Average

People who have yet to pass the bar after two attempts tend to either get real serious about passing the next one or they withdraw emotionally and just go through the motions. Sometimes all it takes is the shock of two failures for those who get serious, to realize that their first one was no fluke. This can cause them to stop, assess and change their ways.

Jonah P.

Jonah was a very popular student, especially with the opposite sex. He liked the good life and was able to maintain it, even through law school, which he crammed his way through. He wasn't surprised by his first bar exam failure, after all, he hadn't studied at all for it. His second failure did surprise him because he thought that his "cram approach to bar passage" would get him over. It did not. Having missed this second time by only a few points, Jonah decided it was time to study. Not only did he really study the third time, he found a study-buddy and the two of them took practice exams under simulated conditions. He passed.

Another student needed a little outside help in getting serious.

Mark S.

Mark was from a very prominent family of achievers. His mother was a high-ranking government official and his father was a law professor. His sister was a cardiologist and his younger brother was an accomplished violinist. While Mark did have to contend with pressure to achieve; he also liked the idea of "poor Mark." That status kept him the center of attention and it kept him out of the "real" world, where he would be forced to meet real demands, for the months of each year he studied for the bar exams. After some "straight" talk between me and Mark, he was able to change his ways to pass the next exam.

That straight talk helped Mark to see how invested he was in his failure. It allowed him to divert attention from the family stars *to himself.* As he realized that he too could shine (in a constructive way), he let go of the behavior which caused him to fail and adopted the attitude and discipline needed to pass.

More self-reflection is needed for those students who choose merely to go through the motions of preparing for the bar exam, or for those who have stopped trying. The typical areas of self-reflection are often embodied in the following questions:

1. *Do you take the exam too seriously?* You are consumed by the thought of failing the exam. You've become a drag to all around you because you do nothing but obsess over the exam and your inability to pass it. When you study, you do not pace yourself; so you find yourself studying for days and then sleeping for days. As the exam approaches, you do nothing but study every waking hour. You were so tired for one exam that you actually fell asleep right there as you read essay question number three (true story).

2. *Do you allow yourself to be distracted?* You do anything not to study—you became obsessed with talk shows; adopted the counselor role in friend's marital problems; and became engaged (why you did this is another story).

3. *Does "something" always happen?* Your "significant other" wanted more attention; your brother got arrested; your in-laws came to visit; your child was hospitalized; and your dog got sick after eating your lecture notes.

4. *Do you really want to be a lawyer?* You had to maintain the family tradition—Papa/mama, grandpa too, were all lawyers; you are the first professional in the family; you really wanted to be a journalist, but they don't make "real" money, or a doctor, but it takes too long and you're not good at math. This last question holds special meaning for the chronic repeater.

Ellen A.

Ellen came to see me right after learning that she had failed the bar exam for a fourth time. At our meeting, I found her to be a very bright, articulate, organized woman, who was a paralegal in a major law firm.

After talking about the exam for a while, Ellen described her family to me, calling them "working class." She stated that she lived with her father and brother, her mother having died years ago. In response to my probing about whether they supported her career goal, Ellen admitted that they would subtly and, sometimes, not so subtly, remind her that she was not smart enough to be a lawyer and that her failure of the exam was positive proof of that "fact."

Before Ellen began her study for the next exam, we looked at the question, *"Do I really want to be a lawyer?"* The answer to this question is just as important for students whose families and friends expect them to become lawyers as it is for students, like Ellen, whose families expect them to fail or who talk about failure in a misguided attempt to protect a family member against future disappointment. Either way, the student must also address the question: *"How many people will I take into the exam room with me?"*

These are such crucial questions because you have to *want* the *prize* to be gained at the end the process—to be a member of the Bar. Otherwise, it is not worth the time and effort you must put into getting it. If you really don't want it, and for whatever reasons, can't come right out and say it, your test scores will say it for you. If this is you, stop the cycle by getting off. Your law degree and the legal education which you have received will hold you in good stead as you search for whatever it is you really want to do.

If this is not you, find out what it is that is keeping you from keeping your eyes on the prize. In Ellen's case, she took both her father and brother into the exam with her. She had accepted their frustration and fears, added them to her own doubts and produced the result which validated their collective expectation—*failure*. It was only when Ellen decided that the goal of practicing law was both attainable by her and was, indeed, *her* first priority, that she was able to muster the resolve to pass the exam. She was able to put her own doubts in the context of a life of achievement and to set up a mechanism to prevent her family's low expectations from bringing her down.

For others, it might just be that they *have yet to swallow "the spinach."* Remember the old *Popeye* cartoon. When he had had enough of Blutto's bullying, he would pop open a can of spinach and say, *"That's all I cans stand. I can't stands no more!"* You have to get to the point where you're sick and tired of being sick and tired. You're tired of the *"poor me"* treatment; of the whispers; of the inertia in your career; and of the time and money you've devoted to the *rite* of passing the bar. Some people get to this point sooner than others; but, if you are still failing the exam, you must eventually get there in order to pass. Reaching that point will mean that you will do *whatever* it takes to pass. You will get out of that dysfunctional relationship. Send your children to sleep away camp. Quit that dead-end job. Stop that compulsive behavior. To pass, we all must eat the *spinach*.

After years of taking and failing the bar exam, it becomes harder and harder to motivate oneself to take it yet another time. Students naturally become depressed (some, in the clinical sense) and fearful. Depressed because nothing seems to work and fearful that the goal of passing will continue to elude them. If you are anything like me, you know the course your depression takes. For me, it is like a downward spiral. If I let it, I will keep going down, down, down. I start to feel sorry for myself. I let my appearance go. I call friends to come to my *"pity me"* party and listen to those *"somebody done somebody wrong"* songs. I can keep this up to the point where I don't want to get out of bed.

But I do. I just make myself do it. Since I know how I can get, I know that I can stop it. I pick a goal, any goal and do it. Eventually, I get back on track. I start by taking *baby steps*, doing little things which will garner little successes and more confidence. I get my nails done. I make lists of things to do and cross them off after I've done them. I begin to surround myself again with affirming people. I call my sister Veronica who refuses to come to my *pity-me* parties. She'll give me an inspirational talk that I'll hate to hear but will desperately need to get motivated. I force myself into one of my routines—usually exercising. From those actions, I allow my attitude to go from *"I can't"* to *"I can,"* from *"I won't"* to *"I will"* and the spiral turns upward. Find someone like Veronica for yourself. He/she may be in your family, at your temple, at a hotline number. Find that person and reach out whenever you need help eating *the spinach*.

If perfectionism is your problem, before you begin exam preparation again, make sure that you have sufficiently mourned the loss of that part of your ego which had never failed anything before. Accept your mortality, your humanity, your imperfection. Don't try to keep your failure a secret! Since we all fail at something at some time in our lives, you are not alone; and like most of us, you will live. In fact, the way we live offers evidence of what we have learned from failure. For some, it is quite a relief. Being perfect is not easy. Now everyone will know that you cannot be everything to everybody and you can begin breathing and living your life more fully. For perfectionists, failure can be a beginning.

So, What If You Fail?

The envelope is thin. A thick envelope is supposed to mean that you passed because they send all the papers needed to complete the admissions process along with your notification letter. Yours, however, is thin. You open the letter and you see a computerized printout with your scores and a cryptic message that you failed.

Now you cry. You deserve it. Hit the pillow, yell at the walls and allow yourself a full measure of the *"if onlys."* *If only I had studied harder. If only I had not gone to those parties. If only I didn't have to work. If only my sister had not gotten sick! If only I hadn't taken two exams*. There are as many *if onlys* as there are people who fail the exam.

So, go through your list of them. When you finish, move quickly to review your exam. It is important to review your exam, no matter how painful. You will never know what you may find unless you review. One of my students discovered that a grader had not marked an entire essay because of the student's handwriting. He successfully appealed that "oversight." A review of your answer will give you valuable feedback on the way in which you responded to the pressure of the exam, as well as identifying your weak subject areas and possible poor exam techniques. Some jurisdictions will provide you with a copy of your answers. New York recently adopted this practice. Others may require that you go to preset locations. Check your state's practice. See *Appendix B* for a listing. Avail yourself of the opportunity if provided.

Always have someone else review your answers along with you. You need an objective assessment of what you did right and what you did wrong. If you review alone, you will compare your answers with the model ones and, like most people, see little or no difference. Someone less invested in the process should review it with you. Some jurisdictions will require that any person accompanying a candidate to a review session be admitted in that state and have no affiliation with a bar review course. A colleague will sometimes go with you. If not, some bar associations may find someone for you. If you can afford it, it is worth the investment to retain an attorney who reviews exams, usually as a side job. These services are listed in legal periodicals, or can be located through the bar review courses.

Your notification letter will tell you *how and whether* you may review the exam. When you do engage in this review, take your time. Review each and every question, and model answers provided to you by the examiners. Note the patterns of the questions and the patterns of the model answers. They generally do not change. Take as many notes as you possibly can and incorporate as much as you can in your study routine.

To Appeal Or Not To Appeal

Depending upon availability, you must decide whether to appeal. Your score generally has to be within a range to be considered. The trend now seems to be automatic appeals. Check your jurisdiction. In some jurisdictions, appeals may involve risk as the end result can be that you lose points. Moreover, as most successful appeals occur where only a point or two was needed to pass, you should not view the appeal of an exam with greater disparities with much, if any, optimism.

If you decide to appeal, your papers should present clear and convincing arguments supporting your assertion of error in law or grading, and why you should receive additional points. Be concise and persuasive, not windy and argumentative. The tone of your appeal may count as much as the substance.

The Next Exam

Once you have decided to take the exam again, the next question is *when?* Given the schedule of exams in many states, you cannot wait for the results of an appeal before you have to begin studying for the next exam. Many people try to avoid the winter exam because it typically has a significantly lower pass rate than the summer exam. If your job depends upon your admission, the decision is made for you. You must take the next exam. If you can wait to take the exam with the higher pass rate, you may fare better from the extra time, as long as you do what's necessary to avoid getting stale.

Good planning is even more important on subsequent attempts than it was on the first one. You are more likely to be working full time. Scheduling and organizing, therefore, become even more crucial.

Should you take a bar review course again? Generally, not, especially if money will be tight during this period. Some courses allow students who are sitting again for the exam to repeat their course for little or no charge. Do so if you have the time and money, if for no other reason than it provides an external structure that some people need.

If you cannot afford the course again, don't worry about it. If your notes are not good, get a friend's notes and books. There is often an underground of people who seem to have everything you might ever want to use to study for the bar exam. Find them. Each local school has one such graduate. A little investigative work will reap great benefits. These people tend to have old and new notes, outlines, old bar exams and MBEs, and sometimes, predictions of exam questions to come. *Just make sure that the law has not changed before relying on old materials.*

When you are ready to begin studying again, take out your notes from your review of the exam. Gear your study to those areas that indicate weakness and emphasize those areas in your study routine. You must not neglect the other areas, because no matter how strong you were in them, unless reviewed, they may show up as weaknesses on the next exam. Thus, if you received a low score on the MBE, take as many practice questions daily as you have to until you reach a passing score. You must also simulate the conditions under which you will take the MBE, i.c., two full sessions of one hundred questions each.

*　　　*　　　*

I recently met a law school classmate of mine who was almost delirious at having passed the bar after trying six times. I asked him what made the difference. His response was simple: *"I got tired of failing. I joined AA."* He ate the spinach. Many people who pass on their next attempt after multiple failures will tell you that they changed their study habits, their approach to the exam, and aspects of their lives. For one student, it was doing more essays; for another it was moving out of his mother's home; and for still another it was after adopting a child. For you, it might not require drastic changes, or dramatic personal decisions, but then again, it just might. The key to success, however, is the commitment to do whatever it takes.

With your bar exam materials in hand, an awareness of what went wrong the last time, a schedule which reflects the activities which must be completed and a renewed commitment to doing whatever it takes, you too will be ready to pass the exam the next time. **Remember**: *"It ain't over 'til you win."*

CHAPTER TWELVE

PAST AS PROLOGUE

I am not so hot at finales, codas, farewell addresses. This is a book about a key step in the process of becoming a professional, an attorney. I have gone through that process and learned enough from it to become a coach, tipster, cheerleader, teacher.

Contrary to what you might expect me to say after saying too much about positive thinking, the bar exam is not a metaphor for life. It is a test of your ability to perform as a professional—a test of what you "know," a test of whether you have the *stuff* to perform under extraordinary pressure; a test of your determination to go through everything you have to go through to even take the test, much less pass it and continue to go through what you have to in order to pass it.

In this, you should approach the bar exam like a ritual as opposed to a rite—a very specific, highly sophisticated, elaborate ritual, full of technical minutia carefully contrived by the gatekeepers to test your resolve. Treat them, and the ritual they have created, with the utmost seriousness and respect. Work as hard as you can to perform the task they have set for you. If the exam has done what any ritual worthy of the name accomplishes, you'll look back at this period and the years in law school, like any proud survivor with a sense of accomplishment, achievement and pride.

The exam is a cauldron, a kiln, into which "students" go and from which full-fledged professionals emerge.

WELCOME AND GOOD LUCK!

ACKNOWLEDGMENTS

The author wishes to thank the following individuals and organizations who have provided assistance and comfort during the making of this work: the Honorable Lawrence W. Pierce; the Late Ambassador Franklin H. Williams; Judge Robert Straus, Professor Harry Dodds and Linda Chin, Esq.; Ed Hinds and Donna Cupid Weeks; Hofstra University Law School; Yvonne Atkinson, Iris Sweeney, Annette Davis, Arthur Springer, Patrick Lee, AGM Graphics, and Quick Byte; Diane Cornelius, Tishalavon Banks, Marie Charles, Roger McCready, and James Miller; Carol Jones; Drs. A.J. Franklin and Nancy Boyd Franklin, Valerie and James Durrah; my family (past and present) and friends. And above all, *I give thanks to the Creator.*

Books on the Bar Exam

Adachi, J. 1990. *Bar Breaker*. Survival Series Publishing, (For the California bar exam).

Gallagher, M.C. 1991. *Scoring High on Bar Exam Essays*. Prentice Hall.

Walton, K.A. 1989. *Strategies and Tactics for the Multistate Bar Exam*. Law in a Flash.

Whitman, R. 1978. *Preparations for the Bar Exam*. Monarch Press.

Books on Test Taking and Studying

Buzman, T. 1983. *Use Both Sides of Your Brain*. Dutton.

Fry, R. 1991. *How to Study*. Career Press.

Gibbs, J. J. 1990. *Dancing With Your Books: The Zen Way Of Study*. Plume.

Gifford, C.S. 1988. *Test-taking Made Easier: How To Win The Test Taking Race*. Interstate Printers & Publishers.

Gilbert, S.D. 1983. *How to Take Tests*. Morrow Press.

Huff, D. 1961. *Score: The Strategies Of Taking Tests*. Apple Century Press.

Rubens, B.G. 1972. *Law Exams*. Law Distributors.

Simon, S.B. 1988. *Getting Unstuck: Breaking Through Your Barriers To Change*. Warner Books.

Thelen, J.N. and Itzkowitz L. 1983. *How to Be a Better Test Taker*. Scholastic Book Services.

Books to Motivate and Inspire

Bloch, E. 1986. *The Principle of Hope*. MIT Press.

Copage, E.V. 1993. *Black Pearls: Affirmations, Meditations, and Inspiration for African-Americans*. Morrow.

Kast, V. 1991. *Joy, Inspiration, and Hope*. Texas A&M Univ. Press.

Lupin, M. 1980. *Peace, Harmony and Awareness*. Teachers Resources Corp.

Peale, N.V. 1970. *Power of Positive Thinking*. Gibson.

Whitman, E.A. 1976. *Meditation*. Simon & Schuster.

Books on Stress Reduction

Fried, R. 1990. *The Breath Connection: How To Reduce Stress-Related Disorders With Easy-To-Do Breathing Exercises.* Insight Books.

Girdano, D. A. 1993. *Controlling Stress & Tension: A Holistic Approach.* Prentice Hall.

Newman, J.E. 1992. *How to Stay Cool, Calm and Collected When the Pressure's On.* American Management Assoc.

APPENDIX B   **85**
General Information on Bar Admissions and Examinations
(Always check with local authorities for the most up-to-date information)

ALABAMA
Board of Bar Examiners
415 Dexter Avenue
P.O. Box 671
Montgomery, Alabama 36101
(334) 269-1515

Disseminated Information:	Rules Governing Admission to the Alabama State Bar; Instructions and Application for Admission to the Alabama State Bar; NCBE Character & Fitness Application and Instructions.
General Provisions:	To be admitted, applicant must meet pre-legal and legal educational requirements; pass the bar exam, the MPRE, and review by the Character and Fitness Committee.
Bar Exam Schedule:	Given twice a year, usually on the last Monday, Tuesday, and Wednesday in February and July. The essay examinations are held on Monday and Tuesday and the Multistate is held on Wednesday. Filing fees range from $260-$460, depending upon residency.
Passing Score:	128 (combined).
Appeals:	None. Applicants who score between 125-127 will automatically be regraded (by the same graders). Failing applicants receive their MBE, essay and combined scores within 60 days of receiving bar results and are allowed to examine their test and the three top papers at State Bar Headquarters. For a $5 fee per exam section, failing applicants can obtain copies of their answers and model answers.

ALASKA
Alaska Bar Association
P.O. Box 100279
Anchorage, Alaska 99510-0279
(907) 272-7469

Disseminated Information: An Admission Application; Instructions for applicants; and Alaska Admission Rules.

General Provisions: To be admitted, applicant must have a J.D. or LL.B degree by a law school which is approved by ABA; be 18 years or older; and be of good moral character; pass the bar exam and the MPRE.

Bar Exam Schedule: Given twice a year in February and July over two and one-half days. One and one-half days are devoted to essays and the other day is the MBE. The essay exam is given in three—3 hr parts. The first part consists of 3 essays, the second part has 6 essays, and the third part is a research-analysis task which will assess how well an applicant can evaluate the effect of various facts, statutes, and caselaw on a client's case. Filing fee is $700.

Passing Score: 140 (combined).

Appeals: No appeal process. Unsuccessful applicants may review their exams.

ARIZONA
Arizona Committee on Examination
Supreme Court of Arizona
111 W. Monroe
Phoenix, Arizona 85003-1742
(602) 340-7295

Disseminated Information:	Supreme Court of Arizona Rules For Admission of Applicants Booklet and Arizona Bar Exam Fact Sheet.
General Provisions:	To be admitted, applicant must meet pre-legal and legal educational requirements; pass the bar exam, the MPRE and Character and Fitness Screening.
Bar Exam Schedule:	Given twice a year in February and July, usually on the last Tuesday and Wednesday. The essay exam is on Tuesday and the Multistate is on Wednesday. Filing fees range from $300-$450, depending on filing date. Character and fitness fees are between $75-200, depending on years out of law school.
Passing Score:	410 (combined).
Appeals:	Within 20 days after notice, unsuccessful applicants may make formal petition for review of their exams pursuant to Arizona Supreme Court Rules. The petition must state specifically the alleged error(s) in grading. The exam may be retaken only **3 times** except in special situations.

ARKANSAS
Arkansas State Board of Law Examiners
Justice Building
625 Marshall
Little Rock, Arkansas 72201
(501) 374-1855

Disseminated Information:	Arkansas Bar Examination Requirements and Information Sheet; Supreme Court Rules gov-

erning Admission to the Bar; Instruction Sheet for Preparation of Character and Fitness Questionnaire; and Character and Fitness Questionnaire.

General Provisions:

To be admitted, applicant must be at least 21 years old; be of good moral character; have received legal training at an accredited ABA law school; and pass the bar exam and the MPRE.

Bar Exam Schedule:

Given twice a year in February and July, usually on the last Tuesday and Wednesday. The essay exam (which counts for two-thirds of score) is on Tuesday and the Multistate (one-third) is on Wednesday. Filing fee is $175.

Passing Score:

75% (combined).

Appeals:

Contact the Secretary of the State Board of Law Examiners at the telephone number listed above.

CALIFORNIA
**The Office of Admissions
of The State Bar of California
1149 South Hill Street-4th floor
Los Angeles, California 90015
(213) 765-1500**

Disseminated Information:

Application for Determination of Moral Character; Schedule of Fees; Bar Exam Schedule: Study Aid Order Form; and Rules regulating Admission to Practice Law in California.

General Provisions:

To be admitted, applicant must be at least 18 years old; be of good moral character; satisfy pre-legal and legal educational requirements; pass the First-Year Law Student's Examination (unless exempted); and pass the bar exam, the MPRE, and Character and Fitness screening.

Bar Exam Schedule: Given twice a year in February and July, over three days to be announced in advance by the Committee. The exam consists of the MBE, essay questions and performance tests as selected by the Board. Filing fee is $325.

Passing Score: Changes from exam to exam.

Appeals: None specified for failed exam. Applicants may appeal an adverse moral character decision.

COLORADO
Colorado Board of Law Examiners
600 17th Street, Suite 520-South
Denver, Colorado 80202
(303) 893-8096

Disseminated Information: General Information Sheet about admission to the Colorado State Bar. Interested applicants must send $10 to the above address to receive application materials.

General Provisions: To be admitted, applicant must have attended an accredited law school and pass the bar exam and the MPRE.

Bar Exam Schedule: Given twice a year in February and July. Filing fees are $200, if first admission; $300 otherwise.

Passing Score: 276 (combined).

Appeals: None specified.

CONNECTICUT
Connecticut Bar Examining Committee
287 Main Street, 2nd Floor, Suite 1
East Hartford, Connecticut 06118-1885
(203) 568-3450 (informational recording) or 568-3762

Disseminated Information: Information booklet for admission to the Con-
                                    necticut Bar. Application fee is $75.

General Provisions: To be admitted, applicant must be at least 18
                                    years of age; be a citizen of the United States;
                                    have satisfied pre-legal and legal educational
                                    requirements; be a person of good moral char-
                                    acter; and pass the bar exam and the MPRE.

Bar Exam Schedule: Given twice a year in February and July on
                                    the last Wednesday and Thursday. Filing fee
                                    is $275.

Passing Score: 264 (combined).

Appeals: None. Applicants who fail the bar will have
                                    the opportunity to review their test results.

DELAWARE
Delaware Board of Bar Examiners
3 West 9th Street, Suite 300B
Wilmington, Delaware 19801
(302) 658-7309

Disseminated Information: Rules of the Board of Bar Examiners of the
                                    State of Delaware.

General Provisions:	To be admitted, applicant must satisfy pre-legal and legal educational requirements; be a person of good moral character; and pass the bar exam and the MPRE.
Bar Exam Schedule:	Given each year on such days as the Board shall designate. Consists of 12 essays and 4 ethics questions. Filing fees range from $275-$375.
Passing Score:	65 (essays), 130 (MBE). Applicant must receive passing scores on 7 of the 12 essays.
Appeals:	Applicants who fail the bar may file a Petition for Review 30 days after the results of the exam are released. Unsuccessful applicants will only be given **3 chances** to pass the exam.

DISTRICT OF COLUMBIA
Committee on Admissions
500 Indiana, N.W. Room 4200
Washington, D.C. 20001
(202) 879-2710

Disseminated Information:	Rules of the District of Columbia Court of Appeals and application information.
General Provisions:	To be admitted, applicant must have a J.D. or LL.B degree by a law school which is approved by the ABA. May be admitted without taking D.C. exam, if passed exam of another jurisdiction. Filing fee is $100.
Bar Exam Schedule:	Given twice a year in July and February. Consists of essays and MBE
Passing Score:	266 (combined).

Appeals: None specified.

FLORIDA
Florida Board of Bar Examiners
1891 Eider Court
Tallahassee, Florida 32399-1750
(904) 487-1292

Disseminated Information: Rules of the Supreme Court of Florida Relating to Admissions to the Bar.

General Provisions: To be admitted, applicant must satisfy pre-legal and legal educational requirements; be of good moral character; and pass the bar exam and the MPRE.

Bar Exam Schedule: Given twice a year in February and July on two successive days. Filing fees range from $725-$1200, depending upon years in practice. Law student registration may result in discounts.

Passing Score: 131 (combined).

Appeals: None.

GEORGIA
Supreme Court of Georgia
Office of Bar Admissions
P.O. Box 38466
Atlanta, Georgia 30334
(404) 656-3490

Disseminated Information: Rules Governing Admission to Practice Law in the State of Georgia; Bar Application; and

Character and Fitness Application.

General Provisions:

To be admitted, applicant must satisfy pre-legal and legal education requirements; receive a certificate of character and fitness to practice law; pass the bar exam and the MPRE.

Bar Exam Schedule:

Given twice a year in February and July on two successive days. Filing fees range from $300-$1100.

Passing Score:

70 (combined).

Appeals:

None. Applicants who fail will have opportunity to review test results.

GUAM
Board of Law Examiners
Guam Judicial Center
120 West O'Brien Drive
Agana, Guam 96910
(671) 475-3199

Disseminated Information:

Schedule/Information and Instructions; NCBE Request for Character Report; Applicant Questionnaire Form; Rules of Admission; Fingerprint Chart; MBE and MPRE Information Booklets; Checklist.

General Provisions:

To be admitted, applicant must be at least 18 years old; be of good moral character, having never been convicted of a felony or crime of moral turpitude; meet educational requirements; and pass the bar exam and the MPRE.

Bar Exam Schedule:

Usually given twice a year in February and July over a three-day period. The MBE is given on the first; the essay is on the second day and the MPRE may be taken on the third. Applicants will be given up to 12 essays to answer on the second day, from which he/she must answer 8. Filing fee is $350.

Passing Score: 132.5 (combined).

Appeals: Applicant failing the exam may appeal by filing a written request for review.

HAWAI'I
Board of Examiners
Supreme Court of Hawai'i
P.O. Box 2560
Honolulu, Hawai'i 96804
(808) 539-4907

Disseminated Information: General Information Sheet on Admission to the Hawai'i Bar and Rules of the Supreme Court of Hawai'i relating to bar admission. To receive application, send self-addressed, stamped envelope ($3.00 for a U.S. address; $10.00 for a foreign address) to: Bar Application, Board of Examiners, Supreme Court of Hawai'i, Ali'iolani Hale, 417 South King Street, Honolulu, Hawai'i 96813.

General Provisions: To be admitted, applicant must satisfy pre-legal and legal educational requirements; receive a certificate of character and fitness to practice law; and pass bar exam and the MPRE.

Bar Exam Schedule: Given twice a year in February and July on three consecutive days. The exam consists of an essay portion, which includes the Multistate Essay Examination (MEE); and the MBE.

Filing fee is $300. Fees for character and fitness screening range from $75-$300.

Passing Score:

Call above number.

Appeals:

Applicants who fail will have opportunity to review test results.

IDAHO
Idaho State Bar
P.O. Box 895
Boise, Idaho 83701
(208) 334-4500

Disseminated Information:

Admissions Information Sheet and Idaho Bar Commission Rules Governing Admission to Practice and Membership in the Idaho State Bar.

General Provisions:

To be admitted, applicant must be a graduate of an ABA-approved law school; pass character and fitness screening, the bar exam and the MPRE.

Bar Exam Schedule:

Given twice a year in February and July on the last Tuesday and Wednesday. The essay and Multistate Essay Examination (MEE) count for two-thirds of score; the MBE is one-third. Filing fee is $350 for students; $500 for attorneys. There is a $40 fingerprint processing fee.

Passing Score:

70% of the highest possible grade as determined by Bar Examination Grading Standards and Procedures.

Appeals:

None. Applicants who fail will have opportunity to review test results.

ILLINOIS
Illinois Board of Admissions to the Bar
430 First of America Center
Springfield, Illinois 62701
(217) 522-5917

Disseminated Information:	Rules Governing Admission to the Bar of Illinois and names of bar review courses in Illinois.
General Provisions:	To be admitted, applicant must be at least 21 years old; be of good moral character and general fitness to practice law; have satisfactorily completed pre-legal and legal educational requirements; and pass the bar exam and the MPRE.
Bar Exam Schedule:	Given twice a year in February and July on the last Tuesday and Wednesday. Filing fee is $300; $150, if pre-registered.
Passing Score:	None specified. Applicants receive only a "Pass/Fail."
Appeals:	None. Applicants who fail will have opportunity to review test results.

INDIANA
State Board of Law Examiners
Merchants Plaza, South Tower #1070
115 West Washington Street
Indianapolis, Indiana 46204-3417
(317) 232-2552

Disseminated Information:	Rules for Admission to the Bar of Indiana; Instruction Pamphlet for Exam and Character and Fitness Screening; and Bar Exam Schedule and Application.

General Provisions:

To be admitted, applicant must be a graduate of an ABA-approved law school; pass character and fitness interview prior to sitting for exam; and pass the bar exam and the MPRE. **MBE is not given.**

Bar Exam Schedule:

Given twice a year in February and July on the last Thursday and Friday. Essays given on both days. Applicants are required to answer 2 of 3 questions in specified areas. Filing fee is $225.

Passing Score:

175 of 250 (essays).

Appeals:

None specified.

IOWA
Clerk of the Supreme Court
State Capital Building
Des Moines, Iowa 50319
(515) 281-5911

Disseminated Information:

Bar Examination Application and Rules relating to the Admission to the Iowa Bar.

General Provisions:

To be admitted, applicant must be a graduate of an ABA-approved law school; must pass the bar exam and the MPRE; and receive a positive report after a morals and character investigation. **MBE is not given.**

Bar Exam Schedule:

Given twice a year in June (on the second Monday) and January (the third Monday) in either Des Moines or Iowa City. It is given in 5 sessions over two and one-half days. Applicant must answer 5 of 7 questions during each session. Filing fee is $200.

Passing Score: 375 (essays).

Appeals: None specified.

KANSAS
Kansas Board of Law Examiners
Appellate Court Clerk's Office
Kansas Judicial Center, Room 374
301 S.W. 10th Avenue
Topeka, Kansas 66612-1507
(913) 296-8410

Disseminated Information: Rules of the Supreme Court of Kansas Relating to Admission of Attorneys; Application for Bar Exam; and Schedule.

General Provisions: To be admitted, applicant must be a graduate of an ABA-approved law school and pass bar exam and the MPRE. Prior to being granted approval to take the bar examination, the applicant will be investigated by the Board. Permission will not be granted until the investigation is completed.

Bar Exam Schedule: Given twice a year in February and July on the last Tuesday and Wednesday. It consists of the Kansas essay examination and the MBE. Filing fee is $175.

Passing Score: 130 (combined).

Appeals: None specified. Unsuccessful applicants will have opportunity to review essay questions. The exam may be retaken only **4 times,** except in special situations.

KENTUCKY
Kentucky Board of Bar Examiners
1510 Newtown Pike, Suite X
Lexington, Kentucky 40511
(606) 253-2733

Disseminated Information:	Instructions for completing bar application; Character and Fitness Information Sheet; Rules of the Supreme Court of Kentucky relating to bar admission; and Application for Bar Exam and MPRE.
General Provisions:	To be admitted, applicant must be a graduate of an ABA-approved law school; pass character and fitness screening; and pass the bar exam and the MPRE.
Bar Exam Schedule:	Given twice a year in February and July. Filing fee is $575, which includes a $175 investigation fee.
Passing Score:	75% (essays) 132 (MBE).
Appeals:	None specified.

LOUISIANA
Louisiana State Bar Association
601 St. Charles Avenue
New Orleans, Louisiana 70130
(504) 566-1600

Disseminated Information:	Rules Governing Admission to Practice Law in Louisiana; Fact Sheet on bar review courses; and Application for Bar Exam and Character and Fitness.
General Provisions:	To be admitted, applicant must be a graduate

of an ABA-approved law school and pass the bar exam and the MPRE. **MBE is not given.**

Bar Exam Schedule:

Given twice a year in February and July. Applicant must take the written exam which consists of 9 separate subject examinations. The fee is $175.

Passing Score:

70 (essays). Applicant must pass 7 of the 9 separate subject examinations, including 4 Code examinations. An applicant who passes at least 5 separate subject examinations, but who fails 2 or more Code examinations totalling 3, but no more than 4, **conditionally fails.**

Appeals:

None. Applicants who fail will have opportunity to review test results. Applicants who have conditionally failed shall be placed on a Limited Reexamination List for a period not to exceed three (3) years from the first day of the month in which the applicant last sat for essay examination. While on the list, the applicant may sit no more than **twice** for examination, limited to those subjects failed, and shall be given and retain credit for those subjects passed. When the applicant has passed 7 subject examinations, including 4 Code, the applicant shall be classified as having passed.

MAINE
Board of Law Examiners
P.O. Box 30
Augusta, Maine 04332-0030
(207) 623-2464

Disseminated Information:

Request for application form ($20 fee); the

Maine Bar Admission Rules; and Application procedures for Maine Bar Examination.

General Provisions:

To be admitted, applicant must be a graduate of an ABA-approved law school; receive positive report from the Character and Morals committee; and pass the bar exam and the MPRE.

Bar Exam Schedule:

Given twice a year in February and July on the last Tuesday and Wednesday. The first day of the exam will consist of questions selected by the Board. The examination may include the Multistate Essay Examination (MEE). The second day consists of the MBE. Filing fee is $230.

Passing Score:

140 (combined).

Appeals:

None. Applicants who fail will have opportunity to review test results.

MARYLAND
State Board of Law Examiners
Peoples's Resource Center
100 Community Place, Room 1.210
Crownsville, Maryland 21032-2026
(410) 514-7044

Disseminated Information:

Rules Governing Admission to the Bar of Maryland; Bar Exam Schedule: Course Sheet; Application and instructions for Maryland Bar; and General Information Sheet.

General Provisions:

To be admitted, applicant must satisfy pre-legal and legal educational requirement; be at least 18 years old; and pass the bar exam and

Character and Fitness screening. **MPRE is not required**.

Bar Exam Schedule: Given twice a year in February and July on the last Tuesday and Wednesday. The exam consists of the Board's Essay Test and the MBE. Filing fees range from $125- $175, with an additional $90 petition fee.

Passing Score: 280 (combined); 140 essay, 120 MBE.

Appeals: Applicants who fail will have opportunity to review test results.

MASSACHUSETTS
Massachusetts Board of Bar Examiners
77 Franklin Street
Boston, Massachusetts 02110
(617) 482-4466, 4467

Disseminated Information: Information Pamphlet Relating to Admission of Attorneys in Massachusetts.

General Provisions: To be admitted, applicant must be a graduate of an ABA-accredited law school; be of good moral character; and pass bar exam and the MPRE.

Bar Exam Schedule: Given twice a year in February and July. The exam consists of an essay portion and the MBE. Filing fee is $210.

Passing Score: 270 (combined).

Appeals: Applicants who fail will have opportunity to review test results.

MICHIGAN
Michigan State Board of Law Examiners
200 Washington Square, North
Lansing, Michigan 48933
(517) 334-6992

Disseminated Information:	Bar Application Kit.
General Provisions:	To be admitted, applicant must be 18 years old; be of good moral character; have satisfactorily completed pre-legal and legal educational requirements; and pass bar exam. **MPRE will not be required in 1996**.
Bar Exam Schedule:	Given twice a year in February and July on the last Tuesday and Wednesday. The exam consists of two parts: the MBE, and essays prepared under the supervision of the Board. Filing fee is $175. There is an additional $125 investigation fee and $39 fingerprint fee.
Passing Score:	135 (combined).
Appeals:	None.

MINNESOTA
Minnesota State Board of Law Examiners
25 Constitution Avenue, Suite 110
Saint Paul, Minnesota 55155
(612) 297-1800

Disseminated Information:	Rules of the State of Minnesota Supreme Court relating to the Admission to the Bar; Application for Bar Exam; Schedule; Instruction Sheet for completing bar application; Fact Sheet; Character and Fitness Standards Sheet; and Map of bar exam location.

General Provisions: To be admitted, applicant must be 18 years old; possess good moral character; have satisfactorily completed pre-legal and legal educational requirements; and pass the bar exam and the MPRE.

Bar Exam Schedule: Given in February and July on the last Tuesday and Wednesday. Exam consists of essays and the MBE. Filing fees range from $300-$450.

Passing Score: 260 (combined).

Appeals: Failing applicants may file a Petition for Review of exam grades and may appeal after an adverse decision is rendered.

MISSISSIPPI
Mississippi Board of Bar Admissions
656 N. State Street
Gartin Justice Building, 1st floor
Jackson, Mississippi 39202-1449
(601) 354-6055

Disseminated Information: Rules Governing Admission to the Mississippi Bar and Information Sheet on bar review courses.

General Provisions: To be admitted, applicant must be of good moral character; be at least 21 years old; meet pre-legal and legal educational requirements; and pass the bar exam, the MPRE and Character and Fitness screening.

Bar Exam Schedule: Given twice a year in February and July on the last Monday, Tuesday and Wednesday.

One and one-half days are devoted to essays. One half day is the Multistate Essay Examination (MEE). The last day is the MBE. Filing fees range from $325-$525, along with an investigation fee for out-of-state residents, which ranges from $100-$200.

Passing Score: 132 (combined).

Appeals: A failing applicant who has filed a Petition for review will have a right to appeal within 30 days after an adverse decision.

MISSOURI
Missouri Board of Law Examiners
Clerk's Office
Supreme Court of Missouri
207 West High Street
Jefferson City, Missouri 65102
(314) 751-4144

Disseminated Information: Missouri Bar Exam General Information Sheet; Application for Bar Exam and Character and Fitness Screening; Rules Governing Admission to the Missouri Bar; Amendment to Application Form; and Change of Address form.

General Provisions: To be admitted, applicant must be of good moral character; be at least 21 years old; meet pre-legal and legal educational requirements; and pass the bar exam and the MPRE.

Bar Exam Schedule: Given twice a year in February and July over two days. The first day is devoted to the MDE. The other day consists of essays, with one session consisting of questions developed by the Board and the other session consisting of questions from the Multistate Essay Examination (MEE). Filing fee is $200 and the character investigation fee is another $200.

Passing Score: 133 (combined) as of January 1, 1996.

Appeals: Applicants who fail will have opportunity to review test results.

MONTANA
State Bar of Montana
46 North Last Chance Gulch, #2A
Helena, Montana 59624-0577
(406) 442-7660

Disseminated Information: Rules for Admission to the State Bar of Montana. Must send $10 to receive more information and an application.

General Provisions: To be admitted, applicant must be a graduate of an ABA-accredited law school; be certified to take the exam; and pass the bar exam and the MPRE.

Bar Exam Schedule: Given in July on two and one-half consecutive days (Wednesday, Thursday, and Friday). The MBE is administered on Wednesday. Montana essay examinations are on Thursday and Friday. Filing fees range from $100- $200.

Passing Score: None specified for essay. 130 (MBE).

Appeals: None.

NEBRASKA
Nebraska State Bar Commission
635 South 14th Street
Post Office Box 81809
Lincoln, Nebraska 68501-1809
(402) 475-7091 or (800) 927-0017

Disseminated Information:	Information Booklet containing admissions information; Character and Fitness Standards; Law School Educational Program Standards; Policies on Handicapped Applicants; and Application for Examination.
General Provisions:	To be admitted, the applicant must meet educational requirements and pass the bar exam and the MPRE. Applicants meeting these requirements will go through a character and fitness screening by the Bar Commission.
Bar Exam Schedule:	Given twice a year in February and July on the last Tuesday and Wednesday. The first day is the Multistate Essay Examination (MEE). The second day is the MBE. Filing Fee is $250.
Passing Score:	125 (combined).
Appeals:	Applicant must request a hearing before the Bar Commission 30 days after the mailing of notice of failure. The applicant must appear at the hearing for an oral presentation and present a concise written brief setting forth the reasons why the applicant should pass the exam. Commission will advise the applicant of its decision. If the applicant is dissatisfied, he/she may appeal to the Supreme Court within 30 days of receiving the notice.

NEVADA
State Bar of Nevada
201 Las Vegas Boulevard
Suite 200
Las Vegas, Nevada 89101
(702) 382-2200

Disseminated Information: A list of qualifications needed for admission to the state bar. There is a $25 application fee.

General Provisions: To be admitted, applicant must have received a J.D. or equivalent law degree from a school approved by the ABA; be of good moral character and not be subject to any mental disorder; and pass the bar exam and the MPRE.

Bar Exam Schedule: Given in July over three days. It consists of a written portion and the MBE. Filing fees range from $250-$925.

Passing Score: None specified.

Appeals: None specified.

NEW HAMPSHIRE
New Hampshire Supreme Court
Noble Drive
Concord, New Hampshire 03301
(603) 271-2640

Disseminated Information: Information Booklet Regarding the Bar Exam; Schedule for Upcoming Exam and List of Subjects which may be included; MPRE Information; Petition and Questionnaire for Admission to the Bar.

General Provisions: To be admitted, applicant must pass the bar exam and the MPRE; be approved by Supreme Court Committee on Character and Fitness; and have graduated from a ABA-accredited law school. Each newly admitted attorney is required to attend a practical skills course within two years of admission. Failure to do so will result in automatic revocation of license to practice.

Bar Exam Schedule:

Given twice a year in February and July on the last Wednesday and Thursday. The exam includes the MBE on the first day and essays, consisting of 12 questions on the second. Filing fee is $110 for the exam and $125 for the character and fitness investigation.

Passing Score:

280 (combined) or 70% equivalent.

Appeals:

Unsuccessful candidates will receive a breakdown of his/her scores by mail approximately a month after taking the exam. Essays are sent to the Supreme Court Building where they may be examined under the procedures provided by the clerk.

NEW JERSEY
Board of Bar Examiners
CN 973
Trenton, New Jersey 08625
(609) 984-7783

Disseminated Information:

Handbook on Admission to the Bar, containing application, exam information and bar association membership information. Applicant must submit a letter of intent in order to receive application.

General Provisions:

To be admitted, applicant must pass the bar exam and the MPRE (or an approved law school course on ethics); receive a Certification of Character; take the Oath of Admission; and sign the Attorneys Roll.

Bar Exam Schedule:

Given twice a year in February and July on the last Wednesday and Thursday. The first day is the MBE. The second day consists of 6 essays which may require applicants to draft legal instruments and documents. Filing fee is $250.

Passing Score:

133 (combined).

Appeals:

None. There is a regrading process which allows for the rereading of essays with a combined averaged scaled score of 130-135.99 (yes, 135!). If the regrading differs by two or more points on any question, the question is then read once more, this time by the Bar examiner who drafted the question. His/her grade will be final.

NEW MEXICO
New Mexico Bar Examiners
P.O. Drawer R
Santa Fe, New Mexico 87504
(505) 820-7007

Disseminated Information:

Supreme Court Rules Governing Admission to the Bar; Booklet containing Multistate Bar Examination (MBE) information; and Instructions for applicants.

General Provisions:

To be admitted, applicant must pass the bar exam and the MPRE; be a person of good moral character; and be physically and mentally capable of practicing law.

Bar Exam Schedule: Given twice a year in February and July usually on the last Monday before the last Tuesday and Wednesday. Filing fee is $600 for students out of law school less than a year and $800 for those who have been out longer.

Passing Score: 133 (combined).

Appeals: Any applicant who has failed the bar examination but is otherwise qualified for admission may, upon written request within 30 days of notice to the applicant of examination results, cause the Board to review grading to determine the **mathematical accuracy of the scoring** of applicant's examination. No other grounds to appeal are provided.

NEW YORK
New York State Board of Law Examiners
7 Executive Centre Drive
Albany, New York 12203-5195
(518) 452-8700; (in NYS) (800) 342-3335

Disseminated Information: Handbook; Rules of the State Board of Law Examiners; Rules for the Admission of Attorneys and Counselors at Law; Application for Examination; and a recent New York State Bar Exam.

General Provision: To be admitted, applicant must meet education requirements along with passing the bar exam and the MPRE. Applicants meeting these requirements are certified to respective Appellate Divisions of the Supreme Court for

	review by the Committees on Character and Fitness.
Bar Exam Schedule:	Given twice a year in February and July on the last Tuesday and Wednesday in New York City, Albany and Buffalo. The first day is devoted to New York Law and Practice. It consists of two 3-1/2 hour sessions, containing 6 essay questions and 50 multiple choice questions. The second day is the Multistate. Filing fee is $250.
Passing Score:	660 (combined).
Appeals:	New York has adopted a new automatic regrading and combining of scores procedure. Applicants receiving scores of 650-669 (yes, 669!) will have their essays automatically reread by different graders. The average of the two scores will be computed to reach a final (non-appealable) scale score. If the final score is below 660, applicants may receive copies of their responses. Copies of essays will be published within 30 days of the exam and sample answers will be given to anyone who makes a written request and pays a fee of $15.

NORTH CAROLINA
Board of Law Examiners of
North Carolina
208 Fayetteville Street Mall
P.O. Box 2946
Raleigh, North Carolina 27602
(919) 828-4886

Disseminated Information: Application and Instructions to the applicant; Character and Fitness Guidelines; and Information booklet on the Rules Governing Admission to the Practice of Law in North Carolina.

General Provisions: To be admitted, applicant must pass the bar exam and the MPRE (within 24 months of taking the bar exam); be a graduate of an ABA-accredited law school; possess the qualifications of character and general fitness requisite for an attorney; and be of good moral character.

Bar Exam Schedule: Given twice a year in February and July in Raleigh on such dates the Board sets forth year to year. The exam consists of a written portion (60% of score) and the MBE (40%). Filing fee is $400.

Passing Score: None specified.

Appeals: None specified.

NORTH DAKOTA
State Board of Bar Examiners
1st Floor, Judicial Wing
600 East Boulevard Avenue
Bismarck, North Dakota 58505-0530
(701) 328-4201

Disseminated Information: Before the information is provided, applicant must submit a 9" x 12" self-addressed envelope with prepaid postage to the State Bar Board. Applicant then receives a Bar Examination Application; Statutes and Rules Governing Admission to the Bar; a Request for Preparation of a Character Report; and a General Information Sheet.

General Provisions: To be admitted, applicant must meet state educational requirements; be of good moral character; receive a recommendation for admission by the Board; and pass the bar exam and the MPRE.

Bar Exam Schedule: Given only in July on the last Wednesday and Thursday in Grand Forks. The exam is given on two days and consists of the MBE and a essay examination. Filing fee is $50, along with a $175 investigation charge.

Passing Score: 260 (combined).

Appeals: None specified.

NORTHERN MARIANA ISLANDS
Commonwealth Supreme Court
Commonwealth of the Northern
  Mariana Islands
P.O. Box 2165
Saipan, MP 96950
(670) 234-5175, 5176, 5177

Disseminated Information: Application for Admission to the Bar of the Commonwealth of Northern Mariana Islands (CNMI); Bar Exam Information Booklet; and a Public Notice for the Bar Exam.

General Provisions: To be admitted, applicant must be of good moral character, having not been convicted of a felony in the Commonwealth; be a graduate of a law school accredited by the ABA, the

AALS or approved by the Commonwealth's Supreme Court; and pass the bar exam and the MPRE.

Bar Exam Schedule: Given twice a year in February and July on the last Wednesday and Thursday. The first day is the MBE. The second day is essay. There is a morning and afternoon session on each day. Applicants are given up to 12 essays to answer. Filing fee is $150.

Passing Score: 65% (essays), 130 (MBE). Applicant retakes only that part of exam which he/she failed. Passing essay scores will stand for two years.

Appeals: None specified.

OHIO
Admissions Office
Supreme Court of Ohio
30 East Broad Street
Columbus, Ohio 43266-0419
(614) 466-1541

Disseminated Information: Application; Supreme Court Rules for the Admission to the Practice of Law in Ohio; Applicants Character Questionnaire; and Instructions for Registration of Applicants.

General Provisions: To be admitted, applicant must meet state educational requirements; pass the bar exam and the MPRE; and receive a favorable recommendation from the Board of Commissioners on Character and Fitness.

Bar Exam Schedule: Given twice a year in February and July on the last Tuesday, Wednesday and Thursday in

Columbus. The exam consists of essay questions and the MBE. Registration fees range from $30-$130. Filing fee is an additional $150.

Passing Score: 375 (combined).

Appeals: Applicants who achieve total scores of 374 to 374.99 shall have their essays answers regraded. The clerk shall submit the applicant's original essay answers to the Bar Examiners. The applicant's original essay raw score shall be averaged with the essay raw score assigned to the applicant during regrading. These scores will be final.

OKLAHOMA
Oklahoma Board of Bar Examiners
P.O. Box 53036
Oklahoma City, Oklahoma 73152-3036
(405) 524-2365

Disseminated Information: General Bar Information; Rules Governing Admission to the Practice of Law; and Request for Character Report Application.

General Provisions: To be admitted, applicant must pass the bar exam and the MPRE; receive a favorable recommendation from the Oklahoma Board of Bar Examiners; meet state educational requirements; and sign the Roll of Attorneys.

Bar Exam Schedule: Given twice a year in February and July on the last Wednesday and Thursday in Oklahoma City. The first day consists of the MBE (worth 25% of score) and the second day is the essay (75%). Applicant must register with the Board as a law student. Registration fees range from $125-$450. There is an additional exam fee of $250 and an investigation fee ranging between $100-$200.

Passing Score: 2400 (combined).

Appeals: Failing score may be obtained by applicant.

OREGON
Oregon State Board of Bar Examiners
5200 S.W. Meadows Road, P.O. Box 1689
Lake Oswego, Oregon 97035-0889
(503) 620-0222

Disseminated Information: Information Sheet and the Rules for Admission of Attorneys.

General Provisions: To be admitted, applicant must pass the bar exam and the MPRE; be approved for admission by the Supreme Court on moral character and fitness grounds; meet state educational requirements; and execute prescribed oath of office.

Bar Exam Schedule: Given twice a year in February and July on the last Wednesday and Thursday. In addition to the MBE, the exam consists of essay questions, generally based on hypothetical facts, but some questions may take other forms. The Board, in its discretion, may include optional questions. Filing fee is $400, along with an additional $150 investigation fee for admitted attorneys.

Passing Score: 65.000.

Appeals: An applicant who has failed and whose score ranked in the top 30 percent of failing applicants may petition for review of essay answers. The petition must be filed with the State Court Administrator and a copy of the petition served on the Board of Bar Examiners not later than 60 days after the mailing of the notice of failure. The Board will review all petitions and notify the Supreme Court of those who have achieved a passing grade.

PENNSYLVANIA
Pennsylvania Board of Law Examiners
Public Ledger Building-Suite 674
150 S. Independence Mall West
Philadelphia, Pennsylvania 19106-3466
(215) 627-3246

Disseminated Information: Admissions Application; Information Sheet; MBE transfer form; Rules Brochure; and Fee Schedule.

General Provisions: To be admitted, applicant must meet state academic requirements; be of good moral character to practice in the state; and pass the bar exam. **MPRE is not required.**

Bar Exam Schedule: Given twice a year in July and February on the last Tuesday and Wednesday. The first day consists of 8 essay questions developed by Board. The second day is the MBE. Filing fee is $400.

Passing Score: 139 (on both the MBE and essay).

Appeal: None.

PUERTO RICO
Commonwealth of Puerto Rico
Supreme Court
Board of Bar Examiners
P.O. Box 2392
San Juan, Puerto Rico 00902-2392
(809) 725-5030

Disseminated Information: Application packet in Spanish.

General Provisions: To be admitted, applicant must have received a J.D. from a law school accredited by the Council on Higher Education and by the Supreme Court of Puerto Rico if pursued law degree in Puerto Rico, or by the ABA and the Supreme Court of Puerto Rico if pursued law studies outside of Puerto Rico; a good conduct certificate issued by the Police of Puerto Rico within the 90-day period immediately preceding the filing date of application; an informative statement sworn to and subscribed by the applicant, detailing personal history; sworn statements of two attorneys admitted to the bar in Puerto Rico, stating that they know the applicant personally and for how long, and that in their opinion the applicant is a person of good moral character. **MBE is not given. MPRE is not required.**

Bar Exam Schedule: **The bar exam is written in Spanish, but can be answered in English.** The exam is given twice a year in March and September. It consists of multiple choice and essay questions. The essay questions involve factual situations requiring applicant to determine relevant law. The multiple choice and essay questions are developed by a committee of lawyers and law professors. The exam is administered during five, 3-hour periods. Filing fee is a $50 internal revenue stamp and a $1 internal revenue stamp.

Passing Score: 596 out of 1,000 adjusted points.

Appeals: Every student who fails may examine his/her answers to the essay questions, review grading guidelines, and obtain a certified copy of the answers. Thirty (30) days after receiving the detailed grade report, the applicant may petition for reconsideration on the grounds that "manifest error" was committed and that said error was the cause of failure. Reconsideration will be considered by the Board of Examiners.

RHODE ISLAND
Rhode Island Board of Bar Examiners
Clerk of the Supreme Court
250 Benefit Street
Providence, Rhode Island 02903
(401) 277-3274

Disseminated Information: An Application Package and Rules Governing Admission to the Bar.

General Provisions: To be admitted, applicant must pass the bar exam and the MPRE; have graduated from an accredited law school; satisfactorily completed a training course sponsored by the Rhode Island Bar Association either before the bar exam or within a year thereafter; and receive a positive recommendation from the Committee on Character and Fitness.

Bar Exam Schedule:	Given twice a year in February and July on the last Wednesday and Thursday. It consists of the MBE and essay-type questions. Filing fee is $300.
Passing Score:	7 of 12 essays, 140 MBE.
Appeals:	Candidates who fail may file a written request with the Clerk of the Supreme Court for a conference with a member of the Board of Bar Examiners to review answers and grades.

SOUTH CAROLINA
Clerk of the Supreme Court of South Carolina
P.O. Box 11330
Columbia, South Carolina 29211
(803) 734-1080

Disseminated Information:	Application; Rules for the Examination and Administration of Persons to Practice Law in South Carolina; and Instruction Sheet regarding responsibilities once admitted.
General Provisions:	To be admitted, applicant must meet state educational requirements; pass the bar exam and MPRE; be certified by the Committee on Character and Fitness; and successfully complete the "Bridge the Gap" Program sponsored by the South Carolina Bar.
Bar Exam Schedule:	Given twice a year beginning on the last Wednesday of the month in February and July. It consists of 7 sections. Six sections will be developed by the Board Examiners. The seventh is the MBE. Filing fees range from $100-$200.

Passing Score: 70% (essays), 115 (MBE).

Appeals: Those applicants who fail to attain a passing score on any section will automatically have that section regraded using a different color ink. Within 15 days of receiving notification of failure, the applicant may request in writing to the Clerk permission to review examination and the model answers. The MBE portion may not be inspected. The review must take place 30 days after the Clerk receives the request. After reviewing the exam, if the applicant feels there has been an error in the grading, he/she may petition the Supreme Court to have answers regraded by the examiner. The petition must be filed with the Supreme Court within 10 days of the applicant's review of the examination and must enumerate the alleged errors in grading.

SOUTH DAKOTA
Board of Examiners of South Dakota
500 East Capitol Avenue
Pierre, South Dakota 57501
(605) 773-4898

Disseminated Information: Application and Rules and Regulations for Admission to Practice Law in South Dakota.

General Provisions: To be admitted, applicant must have graduated from an ABA-accredited law school; receive a favorable recommendation from the Committee of Character and Fitness; and pass the bar exam and the MPRE.

Bar Exam Schedule: Given twice a year in February and July on the last Tuesday (essays) and Wednesday (MBE) in Pierre. Filing fee is $225.

Passing Score: 130 (combined).

Appeals: None specified.

TENNESSEE
Board of Law Examiners
Nashville City Center
511 Union Street #1420
Nashville, Tennessee 37243-0740
(615) 741-3234

Disseminated Information: Supreme Court Rules for Licensing of Attorneys and Bar Examination Schedule.

General Provisions: To be admitted, applicant must satisfy state educational requirements; pass the bar exam and the MPRE; and receive a favorable character recommendation after investigation by the Board.

Bar Exam Schedule: Given twice a year in February and July on the last Wednesday and Thursday. It includes essay questions, the MBE and other multiple choice questions. Filing fee is $200 if you have resided in Tennessee for the past ten years except for time attending school out of state. The fee is $400 otherwise.

Passing Score. With 125 scaled MBE, applicant must pass 9 of 12 essays; with 130 scaled MBE, must pass

8 of 12 essays and with 135 scaled MBE, must pass 7 of 12 essays.

Appeals: None.

TEXAS
Board of Law Examiners
P.O. Box 13486
Austin, Texas 78711-3486
(512) 463-1621

Disseminated Information: Rules Governing Admission to the Bar of Texas.

General Provisions: To be admitted, applicant must be at least 18 years of age; be of good moral character and fitness; meet state academic requirements; pass the bar exam and the MPRE; file a Declaration of Intention to Study Law; and be willing to take the oath required of Texas attorneys.

Bar Exam Schedule: Given twice a year in February and July on Wednesday, Thursday, and Friday. It consists of the MBE, given on the Wednesday; essay questions given on Thursday; and Procedure and Evidence questions given on Friday morning.   Filing fee is $125 for Texas law students; higher for out-of-state law students and attorneys.

Passing Score: A combined scaled score of 675 out of 1000.

Appeals: Applicants who fail will have opportunity to review test results.

UTAH
Utah State Bar
645 South 200 East-Suite 310

Salt Lake City, Utah 84111-3834
(801) 531-9077

Disseminated Information: Rules Governing Admission to the Utah State Bar. Applications are $15.

General Provisions: To be admitted, applicant must be at least 21 years old; be of good moral character and fitness; pass the bar exam and the MPRE; and have graduated with a J.D., LL.B, or equivalent from an approved law school.

Bar Exam Schedule: Given twice a year in February and July on the last Tuesday and Wednesday. It consists of the MBE and essay component of 12 questions, some of which may be taken from the Multistate Essay Examination (MEE). One essay will deal with Legal Ethics.

Passing Score: 130 (combined).

Appeals: The Board shall review the mathematical accuracy of the scoring upon applicant's written request.

VERMONT
Board of Bar Examiners
109 State Street
Montpelier, Vermont 05609-0702
(802) 828-3281

Disseminated Information: Application; the Rules of Admission to the Bar of the Vermont Supreme Court; sample essay exam questions; and a number of information sheets. An admissions packet costs $15.

General Provisions:

To be admitted, applicant must receive a passing score on the bar exam and the MPRE; meet state educational requirements; receive a favorable recommendation from the Character and Fitness Committee; and be prepared to take the Oath of office.

Bar Exam Schedule:

Given twice a year in July and February on the last Wednesday and Thursday. It consists of an essay portion and the MBE. Filing fee is $240.

Passing Score:

36 (essays), 135 (MBE).

Appeals:

An applicant who has failed the examination may petition to review the results. Within a prescribed time period after review, applicant may appeal to the Chairperson. The appeal shall be in the form of a written petition which shall set forth specifically and in detail any claim of misconduct by an examiner or the Board. If the Chairperson finds such as alleged in the petition, he/she will then forward it to the full Board where a determination will be made and the applicant so notified.

VIRGIN ISLANDS
Territorial Court of the Virgin Islands
Post Office Box 70
St. Thomas, Virgin Islands 00804
(809) 774-7674

Disseminated Information:

Application for Admission; Rule 302—Admission to the Virgin Islands Bar; and Information Sheet.

General Provisions:

To be admitted, applicant must be at least 21 years old; have graduated from an accredited law school approved by the ABA; be recommended by the Bar Committee after an investigation of character; and pass the bar exam and the MPRE.

Bar Exam Schedule:

Given twice a year in February and July on the last Tuesday and Wednesday. It consists of an essay portion and the MBE. The MBE is given on the first day, and the essay on the second. Filing fee is $550.

Passing Score:

70%.

Appeals:

An applicant will be permitted, upon written request, to review and make notes of exam under the supervision of a member of the Committee of Bar Examiners. Upon written request, the applicant may put forth questions, comments, and objections regarding the exam to the Committee of Bar Examiners.

VIRGINIA
Virginia Board of Bar Examiners
Mutual Building-Suite 620
Ninth and Main Streets
Richmond, Virginia 23219
(804) 786-7490

Disseminated Information:

Information Brochure and Schedule of fees.

General Provisions:

To be admitted, applicant must meet state academic requirements; be approved by the Board after a character and fitness screening; and pass the bar exam. **MPRE is not required.**

Bar Exam Schedule:

Given twice a year in February and July on the last Tuesday and Wednesday. It is a two-part exam, given during the morning and afternoon of each day. The first part (Tuesday) is the essay portion. The second part (Wednesday) is the MBE. Filing fees range from $150-$325. The application fee is $275.

Passing Score: 714 (combined).

Appeals: None specified.

WASHINGTON
Washington State Bar Association
2001 Sixth Avenue, Suite 500
Seattle, Washington 98121-2599
(206) 727-8209

Disseminated Information: Information Sheet. There is $10 fee for an application packet.

General Provisions: To be admitted, applicant must be a graduate of an ABA-approved law school; receive a favorable recommendation from the Character and Fitness Committee (you must receive this before you can take the bar exam); and pass the State bar exam. **MBE is not given. MPRE is not required.**

Bar Exam Schedule: Given twice a year in February and July over three days. Each full day includes 6 essay questions to be answered in two sessions. The third day consists of a single hour and fifteen minutes session comprised of 6 short essay questions on Washington Rules of Professional Conduct. Filing fee is $375 for student applicants.

Passing grade: 70%. Applicant must receive passing scores on all parts of the exam. If applicant fails any part, he/she may retake that portion at the next exam.

Appeals: None specified.

WEST VIRGINIA
Law Examiners Board
Building 1 E-400
1900 Kanawha Boulevard East
Charleston, West Virginia 25305-0837
(304) 558-7815

Disseminated Information: West Virginia Rules for Admission to the Prac-
                                     tice of Law; Fee Schedule and Examination
                                     Schedule. There is a $20 application fee.

General Provisions: To be admitted, applicant must be at least 18
                                     years of age; be recognized by the Board as
                                     being of good moral character and fitness;
                                     meet state educational requirements; and pass
                                     the bar exam and the MPRE.

Bar Exam Schedule: Given twice a year in February and July on
                                     the last Tuesday and Wednesday. It consists
                                     of three parts. Part A is the West Virginia Es-
                                     say Examination (WVEE), which includes 7
                                     essay questions of which applicant must an-
                                     swer 6. Part B consists of the Multistate Es-
                                     say Examination (MEE). Part C is the MBE.
                                     Filing fee is $275.

Passing Score: 135 (average).

Appeals: None. Applicant may review exam.

WISCONSIN
Board of Bar Examiners
119 Martin Luther King Boulevard
Room 405

Madison, Wisconsin 53703-3355
(608) 266-9760

Disseminated Information:	Wisconsin Supreme Court Rules—Admission to the Bar. There is a $10 application fee.
General Provisions:	To be admitted, applicant must pass the bar exam; receive a positive recommendation from the Board concerning Character and Fitness; and take the Attorneys Oath. **MPRE is not required.**
Bar Exam Schedule:	Given twice a year in February and July on the last Tuesday and Wednesday. It consists of an essay part and the MBE. Filing fee is $300.
Passing Score:	254 (combined). Applicant must score a minimum of 127 on the essays.
Appeals:	None specified.

WYOMING
Supreme Court of Wyoming
Supreme Court Building
2301 Capitol Avenue
Cheyenne, Wyoming 82002
(307) 777-7316

Disseminated Information:	Application Package; Information Sheet; and the Rules and Procedures Governing Admission to the Practice of Law in Wyoming.
General Provisions:	To be admitted, applicant must pass the bar exam and MPRE; meet state educational requirements; and receive a favorable Charac-

ter and Fitness recommendation from the
Board of Examiners.

Bar Exam Schedule: Given twice a year in February and July. It
                              consists of two parts, essay questions prepared
                              or approved by the Board and the MBE. Fil-
                              ing fee is $200.

Passing score: 70 (essays), 130 (MBE).

Appeals: Applicant may review the essay portion of the
                              exam.

APPENDIX C
Sample Calendars

MAY

SUN.	MON.	TUE.	WED.	THURS.	FRI.	SAT.
	TORTS A.M. Exercise/Family 9-12 Do Torts Essay Review Essay(w/model) 12-1 Lunch 1-3 Read/Outline tonight's lec. MBE 3-6 Travel/mult. choice/MBE 6-10 Bar Review course	**TORTS** A.M. Exercise/Family 9-12 Do Torts Essay & Review 12-1 Lunch 1-3 Read/Outline lec./MBE 3-6 Travel/multi./MBE 6-10 Bar Review course	**EVID** A.M. Exercise/Family 9-12 Do Evid Essay & Review 12-1 Lunch 1-3 Read/Outline lec./MBE 3-6 Travel/multi./MBE 6-10 Bar Review course	**EVID** A.M. Exercise/Family 9-12 Do Evid Essay & Review 12-1 Lunch 1-3 Read/Outline lec./MBE 3-6 Travel/multi./MBE 6-10 Bar Review course	**EVID** A.M. Exercise/Family 9-12 Do Evid Essay & Review 12-1 Lunch 1-3 Read/Outline lec./MBE 3-6 Travel/multi./MBE 6-10 Bar Review course	(SABBATH & FAMILY) AM; Catch up PM: Study Session
(SABBATH & FAMILY) AM; Catch up PM: Study Session	**EVID** A.M. Exercise/Family 9-12 Do Evid Essay & Review 12-1 Lunch 1-3 Read/Outline lec./MBE 3-6 Travel/multi./MBE 6-10 Bar Review course	**CRIM LAW** A.M. Exercise/Family 9-12 Do Crim Essay & Review 12-1 Lunch 1-3 Read/Outline lec./MBE 3-6 Travel/multi./MBE 6-10 Bar Review course	**CRIM LAW** A.M. Exercise/Family 9-12 Do Crim Essay & Review 12-1 Lunch 1-3 Read/Outline lec./MBE 3-6 Travel/multi./MBE 6-10 Bar Review course	**CON LAW** A.M. Exercise/Family 9-12 Do Con Essay & Review 12-1 Lunch 1-3 Read/Outline lec./MBE 3-6 Travel/multi./MBE 6-10 Bar Review course	**CON LAW** A.M. Exercise/Family 9-12 Do Con Essay & Review 12-1 Lunch 1-3 Read/Outline lec./MBE 3-6 Travel/multi./MBE 6-10 Bar Review course	(SABBATH & FAMILY) AM; Catch up PM: Study Session (BILLS DUE)

JUNE

SUN.	MON.	TUE.	WED.	THURS.	FRI.	SAT.
				CON LAW A.M. Exercise/Family 9-12 Do Con Essay & Review 12-1 Lunch 1-3 Read/Outline lec./MBE 3-6 Travel/multi./MBE 6-10 Bar Review course	**CON LAW** A.M. Exercise/Family 9-12 Do Con Essay & Review 12-1 Lunch 1-3 Read/Outline lec./MBE 3-6 Travel/multi./MBE 6-10 Bar Review course	(SABBATH & FAMILY) AM; Catch up PM: Study Session
(SABBATH & FAMILY) AM; Catch up PM: Study Session	**CONFLICTS** A.M. Exercise/Family 9-12 Do Conf. Essay & Review 12-1 Lunch 1-3 Read/Outline lec./MBE 3-6 Travel/multi./MBE 6-10 Bar Review course	**FED JUR** A.M. Exercise/Family 9-12 Do F.J. Essay & Review 12-1 Lunch 1-3 Read/Outline lec./MBE 3-6 Travel/multi./MBE 6-10 Bar Review course	**PROC.** A.M. Exercise/Family 9-12 Do Proc. Essay & Review 12-1 Lunch 1-3 Read/Outline lec./MBE 3-6 Travel/multi./MBE 6-10 Bar Review course	**PROC.** A.M. Exercise/Family 9-12 Do Proc. Essay & Review 12-1 Lunch 1-3 Read/Outline lec./MBE 3-6 Travel/multi./MBE 6-10 Bar Review course	**PROC.** A.M. Exercise/Family 9-12 Do Proc. Essay & Review 12-1 Lunch 1-3 Read/Outline lec./MBE 3-6 Travel/multi./MBE 6-10 Rehearsal dinner	(SABBATH & FAMILY) SISTER'S WEDDING
(SABBATH & FAMILY) MAKE-UP DAY	**PROC.** A.M. Exercise/Family 9-12 Do Proc. Essay & Review 12-1 Lunch 1-3 Read/Outline lec./MBE 3-6 Travel/multi./MBE 6-10 Bar Review course	**UCC.** A.M. Exercise/Family 9-12 Do UCC. Essay & Review 12-1 Lunch 1-3 Read/Outline lec./MBE 3-6 Travel/multi./MBE 6-10 Bar Review course	**SALES** A.M. Exercise/Family 9-12 Do Sales Essay & Review 12-1 Lunch 1-3 Read/Outline lec./MBE 3-6 Travel/multi./MBE 6-10 Bar Review course	**NEGO. INS.** A.M. Exercise/Family 9-12 Do N.I. Essay & Review 12-1 Lunch 1-3 Read/Outline lec./MBE 3-6 Travel/multi./MBE 6-10 Bar Review course	**CORP.** A.M. Exercise/Family 9-12 Do Corp. Essay & Review 12-1 Lunch 1-3 Read/Outline lec./MBE 3-6 Travel/multi./MBE 6-10 Bar Review course	(SABBATH & FAMILY) AM; Catch up PM: Study Session
(SABBATH & FAMILY) AM; Catch up PM: Study Session	**CORP.** A.M. Exercise/Family 9-12 Do Corp. Essay & Review 12-1 Lunch 1-3 Read/Outline lec./MBE 3-6 Travel/multi./MBE 6-10 Bar Review course	**CONTRACTS** A.M. Exercise/Family 9-12 Do Cont. Essay & Review 12-1 Lunch 1-3 Read/Outline lec./MBE 3-6 Travel/multi./MBE 6-10 Bar Review course	**CONTRACTS** A.M. Exercise/Family 9-12 Do Cont. Essay & Review 12-1 Lunch 1-3 Read/Outline lec./MBE 3-6 Travel/multi./MBE 6-10 Bar Review course	**CONTRACTS** A.M. Exercise/Family 9-12 Do Cont. Essay & Review 12-1 Lunch 1-3 Read/Outline lec./MBE 3-6 Travel/multi./MBE 6-10 Bar Review course	**PROPERTY** A.M. Exercise/Family 9-12 Do Prop. Essay & Review 12-1 Lunch 1-3 Read/Outline lec./MBE 3-6 Travel/multi./MBE 6-10 Bar Review course	(SABBATH & FAMILY) AM; Catch up PM: Study Session
(SABBATH & FAMILY) AM; Catch up PM: Study Session	**PROPERTY** A.M. Exercise/Family 9-12 Do Prop. Essay & Review 12-1 Lunch 1-3 Read/Outline lec./MBE 3-6 Travel/multi./MBE 6-10 Bar Review course	**PROPERTY** A.M. Exercise/Family 9-12 Do Prop. Essay & Review 12-1 Lunch 1-3 Read/Outline lec./MBE 3-6 Travel/multi./MBE 6-10 Bar Review course	**TRUST/EST** A.M. Exercise/Family 9-12 Do T&E Essay & Review 12-1 Lunch 1-3 Read/Outline lec./MBE 3-6 Travel/multi./MBE 6-10 Bar Review course	**TRUST/EST** A.M. Exercise/Family 9-12 Do T&E Essay & Review 12-1 Lunch 1-3 Read/Outline lec./MBE 3-6 Travel/multi/MBE 6-10 Bar Review course	**DOM. REL.** A.M. Exercise/Family 9-12 Do Dom. Rel. Essay & Review 12-1 Lunch 1-3 Read/Outline lec./MBE 3-6 Travel/multi./MBE 6-10 Bar Review (Bills Due)	

APPENDIX C
Sample Calendars

JULY

SUN.	MON.	TUE.	WED.	THURS.	FRI.	SAT.
				DOM. REL. A.M. Exercise/ Family 9-12 Do Dom. Rel. Essay & Review 12-1 Lunch 1-3 Read/ Outline lec./MBE 3-6 Travel/ multi. /MBE 6-10 Bar Review	**TAX** A.M. Exercise/ Family 9-12 Do Tax Essay & Review 12-1 Lunch 1-3 Read/ Outline lec./MBE 3-6 Travel/ multi. /MBE 6-10 Bar Review	(SABBATH & FAMILY) AM; Catch up PM: Study Session
(SABBATH & FAMILY) AM; Catch up PM: Study Session	HOLIDAY OFF	**AGENCY/PART** A.M. Exercise/ Family 9-12 Do A.P. Essay & Review 12-1 Lunch 1-3 Read/ Outline lec./MBE 3-6 Travel/ multi. /MBE 6-10 Bar Review Course	**SURETY/AD LAW** A.M. Exercise/ Family 9-12 Do S./AL Essay & Review 12-1 Lunch 1-3 Read/ Outline lec./MBE 3-6 Travel/ multi. /MBE 6-10 Bar Review Course	**BAIL/INSU** A.M. Exercise/ Family 9-12 Do B./I. Essay & Review 12-1 Lunch 1-3 Read/ Outline lec./MBE 3-6 Travel/ multi. /MBE 6-10 Bar Review Course	**MISC.** A.M. Exercise/ Family 9-12 Do Essay & Review 12-1 Lunch 1-3 Read/ Outline lec./MBE 3-6 Travel/ multi. /MBE 6-10 Bar Review Course	(SABBATH & FAMILY) MBE PRACTICE DAY
(SABBATH & FAMILY) MBE PRACTICE DAY	DO OUTLINES/ REVIEW Crimes Crim Proc Evid Torts	DO OUTLINES/ REVIEW Fed. Jur. CPLR Conflicts Corp	DO OUTLINES/ REVIEW Dorm. Rel. T & E	DO OUTLINES/ REVIEW Tax Insur. Bail Surety K	DO OUTLINES/ REVIEW Property Sales & Paper Equity UCC	(SABBATH & FAMILY) MINI BAR EXAM
			(Flex Days)			
(SABBATH & FAMILY) MINI BAR EXAM (KIDS TO MOM'S)	A.M. Exercise/ Family	A.M. Exercise/ Family	A.M. Exercise/ Family	A.M. Exercise/ Family	A.M. Exercise/ Family	(SABBATH & FAMILY)
		PRACTICE EXAMS **(Flex Days)**				
(SABBATH & FAMILY)						VACATION
		Bar Exam Week				

SUN.	MON.	TUE.	WED.	THURS.	FRI.	SAT.

APPENDIX D
Work Calendars

SUN.	MON.	TUE.	WED.	THURS.	FRI.	SAT.

SUN.	MON.	TUE.	WED.	THURS.	FRI.	SAT.

APPENDIX E
Sample Notes
(These notes are presented for form only. Do not rely on law.)

BOOK NOTES
§ 9-11
(1) Suspension: when there are no persons in being by whom an absolute fee or estate in possession (life) can be conveyed or transferred
(2) every present or future is void from its creation if the absolute power of alienation is suspended by any limitation of condition for a life in being at the creation of the estate and 21 yrs. A conceived child is a life being. Life in being must be determined
(b) no estate in property is valid unless it must (by its term or by operation of law) vest if at all, not later than 21 yrs after one or more lives in being at creation of estate and any period of gestation involved.

9-1.2
If estate will not vest because person to attain excess of 21 yrs, 21 yrs will be the age.

9-1.3 Construction
a) these provisions govern
b) creator presumed to have intended a valid estate
c) presumption is that one named in an instruments is a life in being ...

LECTURE NOTES
Rule Of Perpetuities
Before you can sign name to document must be alive. If there is no one around who can sign a document conveying property by deed w/rt to take possession there is a suspension of the power of alienation... no one who can alienate by bill of sale or deed (rule applies to personal as well as real property) e.g. to A for life, B for life, C for life. The absolute power of alienation not suspended as creator has created a reversionary interest in himself by conveying less than his full estate. Any time estate comes back to donor-reversionary interest, e.g.2 A for life, B for life, remainder to A,B,C, all in being, such not equal suspension because all can join to alienate interest in a remainder. The creator of estate gives away everything. Can create possibility of reverter, e.g. to A for life, B for life, remainder to C if C survives A & B. C is contingent remainder man as he must survive A&B in order to take. If he predeceases A or B interest reverts back to creator of estate.

Note: T died on 1/1/76 left surviving A,B,C etc. must identify these people to apply. "in its creation" must determine date estate was created by either inter vivos or testamentary disposition (inter vivos - at date —If will -at date died)
b) "...if measure by lives not in being go to problem find out if trust "pay income to X for life, Y for life" . . .

Sample Outline
(These notes are presented for form only. Do not rely on law.)

LABOR LAW

a) LMRA covers employers and employees: not supervisors or managers, not public employers, domestic, agricultural, employees

b) NLRB: exclusive jurisdiction over representation proceedings, unfair labor practices involving employers whose operating affect interstate commerce. *Findings and conclusions w/r to voter representation, appropriate bargain unit conclusive. Query: appealable to Federal District Court or Court of Appeals?*

c) Statute of limitation

d) provides employer with freedom of choice, however, if pursuant to lawful union security clause, may require joining.

I.   Employer Unfair Labor Practices

a) may not discriminate for or against establishment of a union by threats or force, or promises or inducements, e.g. close down a portion of his operation based on anti-union sentiment (may do so if based on business reasons) or "fist in velvet glove" wherein employer may not unilaterally grant benefits motivated by presence of union organizing among employees.

b) duty to bargain in good faith: to meet a reasonable time and confer w/r to wages, hours and conditions and terms of employment. Not required to make proposals but may not make "take it or leave it" demands. Must bargain over issues (subcontracting) which "have a substantial impact (adverse), upon the working conditions of the bargaining unit employees as a whole" vs "issues which are at the core of entrepreneurial control."

c) successor's duties: purchaser of a business who retains or rehires a majority of his sellers or predecessor's employers and who continues the enterprise in substantially the same form as a successor has an obligation to recognize and bargain with employee's union which existed prior to conveyance. Query: need honor collective bargaining agreement? Note if he has knowledge of uflp committed by predecessor he must correct. *A successor may be bound by the arbitration provisions in his predecessor's collective bargaining agreement in a private lawsuit to compel arbitration: but not on uflp* -more so where there is privity of k. No such duty where there is no identity and substantial continuation of same work force.

d) rights of strikers: 1. economic strikes, that which involves an economic dispute, e.g. terms of collective bargaining agreement. In such cases, the strikers may be permanently replaced but are entitled to reinstatement if they reapply unless obtain equivalent employment elsewhere or employer can justify failure; 2. unfair labor practice involved — entitled to reinstatement upon their unconditional request even if permanent replacements hired 60 days after notice of desire to affect k - cooling off period; . . .

INDEX

NOTES

NOTES

NOTES

NOTES

NOTES

NOTES

NOTES

NOTES